CW00541111

SNOWSHOEING:
MONT BLANC AND THE WESTERN ALPS

ABOUT THE AUTHOR

Hilary Sharp is a British, a qualified Accompagnateur en Montagne, and is based permanently in the village of Vallorcine, near Chamonix Mont Blanc in the French Alps. She runs her own trekking business, Trekking in the Alps, guiding walks in winter and summer. Her love of walking and climbing has taken her to many parts of Europe and further afield. She has been snowshoeing since 1990 and discovers new walks and summits every winter.

Hilary is a regular contributor to *High* magazine, and is the author of *Trekking and Climbing in the Western Alps* published by New Holland in 2002.

Trekking in the Alps
info@trekkinginthealps.com
www.trekkinginthealps.com

SNOWSHOEING:
MONT BLANC AND THE WESTERN ALPS

by
Hilary Sharp

2 POLICE SQUARE, MILNTHORPE, CUMBRIA LA7 7PY
www.cicerone.co.uk

© Hilary Sharp 2002
ISBN 1 85284 376 4
A catalogue record for this book is available from the British Library.

Maps: Jon de Montjoye
Photos: Hilary Sharp except where otherwise credited.
Artwork: Roger Bassett

Dedication
This book is dedicated to Jean François Rouge, 1961–2002

Acknowledgements
Lots of people helped with this book: Jean François Rouge, Chris Patient, Charly Ancey, Rachel Smith and Marc Volorio provided various information; Jonathan Williams of Cicerone believed in my idea; Luisa Dusi was an invaluable help for the Italian walks; Patricia Loffi accompanied me on some wild and strange outings; Francine Pasche trusted me on the glaciers; Steve Jones helped generally, notably with the avalanche information; Bernard Marsigny has been the source of much of my rescue and cold injuries knowledge; Gilles Brunot is my weather expert; Martin Nelisse was willing to discuss the finer technical aspects of snowshoe design; Roger Bassett, Des Clark and Kev Reynolds gave valuable input for the maps, and Roger did the crevasse rescue artwork; Shane Holonitch explained about snowshoe running; Jean Pierre and Chantal Ferlin provided information and photos of their inspiring adventures; many people agreed to be in my photos and remained upright whilst I was shooting; finally, and especially, Jon de Montjoye drew the maps and also proof read, encouraged and put up with the project. Thanks to everyone.

Front cover: Great views of the Mont Blanc massif as seen from the Tête de Balme near Chamonix (Route 28)

AMENDMENT

Snowshoeing – Mont Blanc and the Western Alps,
by Hilary Sharp

Route 19, p122
Revised route grade: 1/2
Revised route aspect: E, N, W, S
Map: new text supersedes route on map p123

(text below replaces the paragraph 'Return to the Col de la Forclaz…')

Return to the Col de la Forclaz but do not take the steep ridge up ahead. Go left (south-west) and down a little in the direction of the ski lifts that you don't actually see, then zigzag up through the forest past the Chalais des Anglais, which is marked on the 1:25,000 map. From here reach a clearing, with the ski pistes on the right, and head up left towards the arête, which is quite narrow and separates the valley of St Gervais from the valley of Chamonix. The arête can be corniced. You can then reach the summit of Prarion. Take the time to stand and stare at the wonderful panorama spread out in front of you. Descend by the same route.

Route 20, p123
Revised route aspect: NW, S
Map: new text supersedes route on map p123

(text below replaces the sentence 'Climb the obvious summit…lift station', p124)

From the Bellevue lift station do not go directly to Mont Lachat. Follow the Tramway de Mont Blanc rail line under the summit to the col on the other side of Mont Lachat and go up in zigzags from here.

CONTENTS

Advice to Readers

Readers are advised that while every effort is taken by the author to ensure the accuracy of this guidebook, changes can occur which may affect the contents. It is advisable to check locally on transport, accommodation, shops, etc, but even rights of way can be altered.
The publisher would welcome notes of any such changes.

Approaching the unnamed summit next to Mont de l'Arpille above Martigny (Route 30)

PREFACE

As the snow falls and winter settles in, the footpaths disappear and the mountains take on a totally different appearance from that of their friendly summer façade, when waymarks show the route and flowers please the eye.

However, walking in the Alps in winter is not impossible, and many pleasures await those who come here appropriately informed and equipped to walk the hills on snowshoes.

The blanket of snow gives the high glaciated peaks a new glistening beauty; it provides a superb medium for animal tracks to be displayed, and there is no longer a need for footpaths, as previously rough and bouldery terrain is often rendered smooth, allowing you to make your own tracks where you like.

In this guide I hope to inspire you to come and discover this fabulous winter world, to explore the delights of making your own track, whether it be in the forests during heavy snowfall, when the silence is palpable and only the occasional footprint shows that life goes on, or on high summits way above the valleys on those frequent winter days when the snow is stable and the sun shining. I hope to share with you the pleasures of the cold, clear alpine air, the solitude away from the busy ski lifts, and the satisfaction of completing a winter alpine walk safely.

On snowshoes you can discover the beauty of the mountains in winter, a world that is more or less inaccessible to the walker equipped only in boots, as the depth of snow above about 1000m often renders walking on foot impracticable, except on specially prepared tracks.

Snowshoeing has come a long way in the last 30 years. From being little known, it has become a major winter activity in the Alps and America, enjoyed by people of all ages and all abilities. Snowshoeing can be practised at many different levels of difficulty – just like summer walking – from beginner walks in the valley to forest rambles, nature outings or summit bids. Many itineraries that in summer might appear modest take on a different dimension in winter, when the snow-cover totally changes the nature of the terrain. Thus, modest non-glaciated summits become fine excursions in the snow, when road access is limited and summer chalets are deserted, leaving a world of silence and magic, inhabited by wildlife whose tracks record their comings and going.

There are no defined parameters, no graded pistes, no times to beat – just you and the snow and wherever you want to go. Whilst many people remain in the valleys, doing relatively easy circuits in the woods, an increasing number are venturing higher, above the treeline to the alpine summer pastures (the true Alps) and beyond.

Figures on the trail returning from the Bec Rond

The selection of walks in this book is inevitably arbitrary and subjective. It reflects my interests, the area where I live, and my vision of snowshoeing. I have tried to choose a wide variety of walks of all levels. Some are better known than others; some are just my favourites. I have included several glaciated hikes, which are excellent, but personally I really feel snowshoes come into their own in the non-glaciated mountains. In the winter any top, however small, can be a fantastic objective, giving superb views and providing solitude and the time to savour the joy of winter in the Alps.

One of my outings this winter sums this up: having walked up to the Emosson lake, the aim was to go on further into the mountains. However, conditions were not suitable and I turned back. Looking around, I wondered what to do next. A small hill above the chapel caught my eye – it would be better than nothing. The ascent proved to be far more interesting than expected, leading in an intriguing spiral ascent to the summit. And what a fantastic spot it was. Enchanted by the views spread out before me I remained for a good hour before tearing myself away and heading down, totally satisfied with what I had done. The summit – Six Jeur – remains for me one of the best snowshoe summits of this winter.

My aim in this guide is to enthuse the keen hill-walker to come and experience the Alps in winter on snowshoes. I want to inspire, to motivate and to give you the knowledge and imagination to find other walks of your own. I hope these walks encourage you to do just that!

Hilary Sharp
Vallorcine, France, 2002

Map Key

ridgeway

rivers/watercourse

snowshoe route

refuge

col

village/habitation

road

parking

spot height

ski lift

national boundary

summit

town

lake

glacier

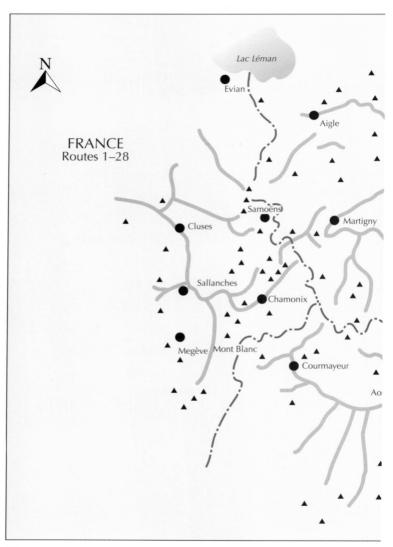

N

Lac Léman

Evian

Aigle

FRANCE
Routes 1–28

Samoëns

Martigny

Cluses

Sallanches

Chamonix

Megève Mont Blanc

Courmayeur

Ao

CHAMONIX AND THE SURROUNDING AREA

Sierre

Sion

Zinal

SWITZERLAND
Routes 29–57

Arolla

Zermatt

Grand Combin   Matterhorn   Monte Rosa

Aosta

ITALY
Routes 58–70

Snowshoeing near the Dent du Géant

GENERAL INFORMATION

HOW TO USE THIS GUIDE

The walks in this guide are designed to be undertaken on snowshoes by those who are properly prepared, given suitable conditions. Compared to summer walking, the additional factors to consider when showshoeing are the cold, the short days and the fact that snow is an extremely variable medium which can change dramatically in a relatively short period of time. For this reason snowshoeing requires a certain knowledge of snow and the associated dangers, as well as the normal requirements for any walk – familiarity with navigation, a working knowledge of first aid and an idea of what constitutes a reasonable day's walk for you.

Whilst you may be keen to skip this introductory information and get straight to the walks, it is essential that you read the sections concerned with safety in winter. Snowshoeing is potentially a very dangerous activity and not one the summer walker should undertake without sufficient knowledge and experience.

Because snowshoeing is a relatively new recreational activity for people who don't live in the Alps, this guide contains detailed information on equipment, technique and safety. The development of equipment reflects the recent interest in snowshoeing challenging terrain, and the last few years have seen a constant and impressive evolution in the design of snowshoes.

The walks themselves (70 in total) are all in sight of (or at least near) Mont Blanc. They are divided into three chapters covering France, Switzerland and Italy. There are walks in the French regions of Savoie and Haute Savoie, the Swiss cantons of Vaud and Valais, and the Italian Valdotain region (i.e. the Val d'Aosta). In each chapter the walks are grouped by region, with each region offering possible bases for snowshoe excursions. There are at least two walks in each area, and many more within driving or bus/train distance. A mountain region offering plenty of walks could therefore provide the base for a one- or two-week holiday.

Near the start of each walk information is presented for start altitude, summit altitude, altitude gain, maps, approximate timing, grade of difficulty and aspect (see relevant sections in 'Practical Information' below). Details are also included of public transport options and any accommodation that may be necessary or optional during the walk itself.

Within each walk section there is information about the walk, type of terrain, views and interesting facts, followed by a description of the route. Any overnights are described, and the telephone numbers for the huts are included, although these can change.

The route of each walk is shown on an accompanying sketch map, some of which cover several walks. It is intended that the route description and sketch map are used in conjunction with the appropriate detailed map(s) of the area.

Other walks will probably occur to you if you look at local maps, and in some instances variations or further options are mentioned (though not described in detail) at the end of the walk description. More ideas can be found by asking at local guides' bureaux and tourist offices. However, do not be tempted to merely follow a snowshoe track when you don't have a map or a guide.

The walks in the guide cover a vast range of terrain from easy, flat valley walks to high mountain expeditions, so there is something of interest for walkers of all abilities in each area of the guide. Whilst each walk is graded, this can only be a loose indication of the level of difficulty. It is crucial to carefully study the map before embarking on any of these walks, taking into account the altitude gain, the length of the walk, the aspect and the surrounding slopes.

Many of these walks can take you into potentially very serious terrain. What may be an easy-to-find trail in summer will probably be invisible in

winter. It is imperative that you have the necessary navigational skills to operate on snow without signposts, waymarks or other indicators of direction. It is essential to be equipped with map and compass and to know how to use them. The maps in this guide are for guidance only not to be used as a navigational tool.

Walkers should be aware that winter conditions are very variable, and snow-cover can change from one year to the next. You need to able to judge for yourself whether it's wise to go up, across or down a certain slope. To do this you must have been trained in avalanche awareness (see p.49), and be prepared to turn back if in doubt.

For the walks on glaciated terrain, you must be experienced in glacier travel (see p.58) or go with a professional. It is vital that you rope up whenever you are on glaciers, even if you can't see any crevasses. You will note that most skiers are not roped up on glaciated ground, but skis provide a considerably larger surface area than snowshoes and in descent move faster, and so the likelihood of skiers falling into crevasses is lower than for someone on foot.

Finally, although all the walks have been checked, things do change, especially in winter conditions. If a slope is not as expected, a track not where it should be, or there is a ski lift not noted in the description, take note of what is found in reality and react accordingly. This guidebook assumes that the walker is

Winter conditions near to Vallorcine

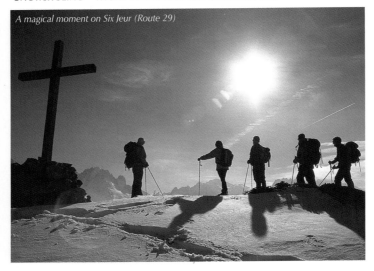

A magical moment on Six Jeur (Route 29)

intelligent, can read a map and use a compass, and will turn back or adjust the walk if necessary.

MONT BLANC

The massif of Mont Blanc is certainly not the most extensive in the Alps – the Monte Rosa massif wins on this score by far – but there is something special about Mont Blanc and its surrounding summits. The highest summit in western Europe, Mont Blanc has recently (October 2001) had its height officially elevated by three metres, and now measures 4810m (15,777ft). Its glaciers are steep and impressive, with the Glacier des Bossons, which descends to Chamonix, claiming the biggest vertical drop of any glacier in the world

(about 3500m). Seen from Chamonix, Mont Blanc is a rounded snowy dome, nothing like as impressive as its neighbours, such as the Aiguille Verte. However, seen from just 30km down the valley from the Aravis range Mont Blanc presents a more pointed summit, clearly towering above all the other peaks. From Italy, it's even more spectacular with its steep rock and ice faces.

Many stories can be told about this mountain, the first ascent being one of them. In 1760 a young botanist, Horace Bénédict de Saussure, travelled from Geneva to Chamonix, no mean feat in those days, to collect samples of alpine plants. Whilst walking in the vicinity of the Brévent, he was transfixed by the view across the valley to Mont Blanc. At this time no one entertained the idea of climbing the alpine summits – only very recently had tourists begun to make the journey to the Alps to see the glaciers, and it was firmly believed that the lofty summits were home to dragons and that anyone who ventured too high faced certain death. The only people with any knowledge of the higher ground were the crystal searchers and chamois hunters, and they stayed well below the tops, always returning to safe terrain before nightfall.

De Saussure decided that he absolutely wanted to stand on the summit of Mont Blanc, and to this end he offered a reward to the first person who could the find a way up for him. The locals of Chamonix initially showed some interest in this potentially lucrative venture, but several futile efforts rather dampened their enthusiasm. Twenty-six years later the reward was still awaiting collection, and Horace the fulfilment of his dream.

One major obstacle was the widely held belief that it would be fatal to spend a night out on a glacier. This meant that all attempts had to return to non-glaciated ground before nightfall, and there was not enough time to reconnoitre a route in the space of one day. Still, sporadic forays continued, and in 1786 one of these featured Jacques Balmat, a young crystal searcher from Chamonix.

A loner with few friends, Balmat had tagged along with a group who were investigating the possibility of reaching the summit via the Dôme de Gouter. As dusk drew in they hurried back down past the Grands Mulets towards the safety of the Montagne de la Côte. However, Balmat had lingered high up near the Grand Plateau – possibly looking for crystals or the route to the top – and when he came to descend he found that fresh snow covered the tracks of the party and that it was fast becoming dark. Realising that it was safer to stay put than risk falling in a crevasse in the dark he settled down for a cold bivouac.

Quite what happened next has remained uncertain. On his return to Chamonix Balmat claimed that he had spied a route to the summit. Later he maintained that he had actually ascended to within metres of the top, but didn't continue to the summit as there were no witnesses to his feat. However, since he was home in time for breakfast this does seem unlikely. Yet he was sure he could climb the mountain, and soon talked another aspirant first ascentionist, Doctor Gabriel Paccard, into sharing the venture with him. Paccard's interest was mainly scientific, which suited Balmat very well, as they wouldn't have to share the reward.

The doctor was treating Judith Balmat, Jacques' sick young daughter, which gave the pair ample opportunity to make plans, and as soon as the weather seemed set fair they started

From Chamonix the Mont Blanc massif, in all its glory

out up the Montagne de la Côte, bivvying at the top under a huge boulder, now known as the Gîte à Balmat.

Next day they made their way over the treacherously crevassed Jonction and continued up the Glacier Des Bossons past the Grands Mulets up to the Grand Plateau, where Paccard's hat was blown off and up over the Col de la Brenva into Italy. The Rochers Rouges provided the crux of the route, giving access to the final summit slopes. They reached the top on August 8th at 6.23pm. In Chamonix they were clearly seen through the telescopes trained in anticipation on the summit. Paccard spent about 45 minutes doing several experiments before Balmat insisted they set off down before it got too dark .

On the descent Paccard became snow-blind, due to having climbed for some hours without the protection of

his hat, and had to be guided by Balmat, who was later to claim that the doctor was totally out of his depth on the mountain and that all credit for the ascent should go to Balmat himself.

On their return to Chamonix they had the heroes' welcome they deserved, although poor Judith was never to know the fame her father had earned, having died in the absence of the doctor. Balmat collected his reward (only to lose it on his return in a mugging incident) and in time managed to portray Paccard as purely a passenger on this ascent. For many years this was believed, and the record was only set straight some time after Paccard's death when the people of Chamonix recognised Balmat as having taken too much of the glory. Now the main street in town bears Paccard's name.

As for de Saussure he finally got

his long-awaited wish and stood on the summit of Mont Blanc on August 3rd 1787, after a four-day siege, accompanied by 18 guides, among them Jacques Balmat.

Now a sunny summer's day will often see in excess of 200 people following in those summit footsteps, albeit reaching the summit by different routes. Mont Blanc is a popular ski tour during April and May. It can be ascended on snowshoes too but, given its length as a walk and the short, cold winter days, this is a very long outing reserved only for those who walk very fast and are able to cope with the technicalities and the challenge of the route in winter. For that reason it is not described in this guide.

HISTORY OF SNOWSHOEING

It is impossible to put an exact date on the birth of snowshoeing. Certainly the first people in northern Europe to use some sort of large shoe to enable them to get from place to place in the snow were the inhabitants of the Arctic, such as Siberians, Lapps and Finns. Proof exists from as far back as 2500 BC, but probably bark and planks were used to the same end well before this.

In other areas it is thought that snowshoes were used as a means of transportation in very early times, possibly to travel from Central Asia, Mongolia and the Siberian steppes towards the American continent at the time when the Bering straits were

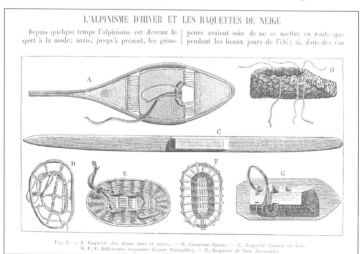

L'ALPINISME D'HIVER ET LES RAQUETTES DE NEIGE

Depuis quelque temps l'alpinisme est devenu le sport à la mode; mais, jusqu'à présent, les grim- | peurs avaient soin de ne se mettre en route que pendant les beaux jours de l'été; si, dans des cas

Fig. 1. — A. Raquette des Alpes (bois et osier). — B. Chausson danois. — C. Raquette danoise en bois D, E, F. Différentes raquettes d'osier (Grenoble). — G. Raquette de bois (Grenoble).

Nineteenth-century snowshoeing equipment. Photo from the Fonds Musée Dauphinois

still a land crossing. This migration took place over many centuries, and some people migrated right down to South America, whilst others, such as the Inuit, stayed in the north. They adapted to the environments in which they had to survive, using materials available to them. Those living in the vast plains are known to have sometimes hunted bison on snowshoes. However, up in the north the Inuit rarely used snowshoes as the snow was often icy or hardened by the wind.

When foreign explorers arrived in America during the 15th and 16th centuries they copied the habits of the native American people that they met. The French particularly embraced the idea of *raquettes*, which they thought resembled the

rackets they used to play *jeu de paume*, the old form of tennis. When fighting the British on American soil during the 17th and 18th century, the French army was equipped with snowshoes.

Unlike many of the native Americans, European alpine people lived mainly from agriculture and cattle. They did not need to get around in winter because they limited their travel during the snowy months. Surprisingly we have no accounts of snowshoes being used by Napoleon I's troops during his battles of the early 18th century, or by smugglers or traders at this time, even though the high passes were fairly frequently crossed during the winter.

It is most likely that the idea for snowshoes in the Alps came from

Photograph of 19th-century snowshoeing. Photo Fonds Musée Dauphinois

Environs de Grenoble
Sommet et chaine du Moucherotte (Hiver)
Papeterie des Alpes Eug. Robert, Grenoble

travellers to America, the early colo-
nials, who on their return adapted the
large American Indian snowshoes to a
smaller version, useful in the Alps for
hunting, for example. The alpine
armies were equipped with snowshoes at the start of the 20th century

In France snowshoes for recre-
ation appeared at the end of the 19th
century, introduced by a Monsieur
Henri Duhamel, who is also credited
with the introduction in the French
Alps of skiing as a leisure activity.

The development of modern
snowshoes took place in France and
America. In France the first modern
snowshoes date from 1975, made by
Baldas in aluminium. In the USA
Tubbs were pioneering in the development of modern shoes.

SNOWSHOE RUNNING

This is becoming quite popular both
in Europe and America, and races are
held throughout the winter, often
sponsored by snowshoe manufacturers. One development has been that
of snowshoes for running, and asym-
metric snowshoes now exist for this.

PREPARED SNOWSHOE TRAILS

In some resorts there are trails specially made for snowshoeing. These
are sometimes groomed tracks, and
they are marked with small snowshoe
signs, are usually of a very easy standard and take about an hour. Ask in
the local tourist offices for details.

ALPAGES

Throughout this book the word
'alpages' is used for want of an
English equivalent. An alpage is a
summer grazing area above the tree-
line used for centuries by alpine farmers as they practise transhumance –
the process of taking cattle to higher
grazing ground as the summer pro-
gresses. In the autumn the cattle
return to the village and are kept
inside for the winter months. The
alpages usually have a few summer
chalets for the farmers, and these are
often used for cheese-making too.

The relevance for snowshoers is
that alpages make a fine objective for
a walk if conditions (yours or that of
the mountains) dictate a shorter walk.
Being above the forests the alpages
benefit from wonderful views of the
surrounding peaks, and are usually
relatively flat areas away from the
steep-sided higher summits. Lucky
walkers may find a sunny terrace
where they can sit and picnic with
their back against the warm wood of
the chalet savouring spectacular
snowy peaks against a backdrop of
bright blue sky – the stuff of dreams.
Or if it's snowing hard the overhang-
ing chalet eaves will provide a welcome respite from the weather whilst
you don yet more warm layers and
grab a quick drink!

SNOWSHOEING AND SKIING

Aside from in the downhill-ski areas,
the ski tourer is the skier you are most
likely to encounter when snowshoeing.

An alpage after fresh snowfall near to Mont de l'Arpile (Route 30)

These people enjoy the mountains for the beauty, tranquillity and wilderness, just like snowshoers, and the two activities can very well exist side by side. Whilst some skiers have yet to appreciate the finer aspects of snowshoeing, and tend to consider it the soft option, they are quickly coming to appreciate its advantage over skis in certain environments – in forests for example – as each year sees snowshoe tracks in higher and wilder places.

When ski tourers skin uphill they usually make a nice double track which is pleasant for those coming after them. If snowshoers use the same track it's not so pleasant for the following skiers, so unless the depth of snow makes it impossibly tiring to

make a snowshoe track, it's best to keep off the ski tracks.

SKI PISTE ETIQUETTE

Hopefully most snowshoe walks keep well away from the ski areas – after all one of the joys of snowshoeing is that you can explore untracked and unfrequented areas. However, some of the ski lifts do give access to great summits; similarly, snowshoe walks may well begin in valleys which have cross-country ski pistes.

In these places it is the walker who is out of place, not the skier: skiers, both downhill and cross-country, have paid for a ski-pass, which partly funds the tracking of pistes. This pass also includes insurance for the piste user. Walkers haven't paid for the privilege of using the piste, unless they've taken the lift, and hence do not have the right to be on it.

Inevitably as you leave a lift you may be obliged to walk on the piste for a little way. In this case keep well to the side in the interests of your own safety – it is somewhat optimistic to think that all skiers can avoid you if you are in the way.

However, the mountains are for everyone, and if you encounter any problems it's important to know the law. In France it is illegal to walk on the pistes, but you cannot receive a fine for being there. In Switzerland I have been unable to find any law prohibiting walkers from the pistes (although some snowshoers have encountered problems), and the legal situation is the same in Italy.

In the case of cross-country pistes there is often a separate walkers' track, but if not you should walk next to, not on, the piste – snowshoes are made for walking in deep snow, and it's much more pleasant to do so rather than walking on a track. If you have to cross a piste be very careful not to step on the pisted tramlines, as this breaks them down and makes it difficult for the cross-country skiers.

SNOWSHOEING AND CHILDREN

Snowshoeing is a great activity for children as long as certain safety factors are taken into consideration.

- The days are short and cold in the depths of winter, so children need to be well-equipped: they

Snowshoeing
is a great activity for children

need good boots and proper warm clothing that they can walk comfortably in.
- The magnificence of the views and the splendour of nature generally interest children for about five seconds maximum, so you need to have other objectives for a snowshoe walk.
- Animal tracks (see p.26) are always interesting to children, and a sledging session also makes a good midday break.
- Children usually have an overpowering need to roll around in

25

Making double tracks en route to the Mont de l'Arpille (Route 30)

snow, but once they've got snow down their clothes they get cold very quickly, so it's best not to plan to stay out too long. You can always play obstacle courses and jumping competitions if there's time and energy to spare at the end of the walk.

- Most manufacturers make snowshoes for kids, but these tend to be basic, so don't try anything too ambitious in terms of terrain.

SIGNS OF WILDLIFE IN THE MOUNTAINS

Although most wild animals are sensible enough to stay well away from the busy ski areas of the Alps, whilst snowshoeing there's every chance you'll see tracks, droppings and even the animals

themselves if you're lucky. There's lots going on in the winter. Most animals do not hibernate and consequently have to work pretty hard to get enough to eat during the harsh winter months. However, marmots and bears do hibernate, so don't expect to see many of these. A lot of activity goes on at dusk and dawn, so by the time you are out showshoeing there may be the telltale scurrying footprints.

Animals such as the mountain hare have a predilection for the edges of forests or boulder fields, where they can quickly find protection if an intruder arrives. The hare's footprints are easily recognised by his characteristic Y-shape formed by the hind legs coming round the sides of his forefeet as he bounds along.

The fox, which gets to most places, even summits of glaciated peaks, makes a track that can be confused with the pine marten or even domestic cats. Look carefully, however, and you'll often see a trace of the fox's tail trailing along behind.

Near to forests and vegetation there are often lots of cloven hoof prints. These could belong to deer, chamois or ibex depending on the terrain. Size obviously gives an indication, as can droppings.

Birds also abound in winter, and you'll probably come across footprints appearing out of nowhere in the snow. These could be made by the ptarmigan, which lives in a hole in the snow – if disturbed it will burst out at the last minute. Normally, however this bird keeps a low profile, perfectly camouflaged in its white winter plumage.

When you find signs of animal life the first consideration is: who are the possible culprits? Secondly, this list is immediately reduced by studying the size, depth and distance between the tracks. These factors give a good idea of the size of the animal, and some candidates will be eliminated. Thirdly, a basic knowledge of the types of tracks produced by different animals will help you to arrive at some conclusion.

Look around for other signs – half-eaten cones and berries, marks on trees, feathers or fur. Everything tells a story, and the more observant you are the more you'll see – even if

The hare's distinctive tracks reveal his nocturnal comings and goings

the animals themselves don't always appear. However, when you do come across animals nibbling at vegetation, lying low or just trying to survive in deep snow, do keep a good distance away. Binoculars allow you to see all you want, but if you get too close and the animal has to run it can use a week's supply of energy wading through deep snow just to get away from you.

It is worth purchasing a book about animal tracks and droppings – numerous books exist on the subject in France, Italy and Switzerland, and this will certainly add a lot to your snowshoe walks.

PRACTICAL INFORMATION

GETTING TO THE ALPS

By Air: The growth of cheap airlines serving Europe has made it a fairly inexpensive proposition to visit the Alps. For the area described in this guide, the airports of Geneva and Turin are the most convenient. There are good train services to the alpine bases. Alternatively taxis from the airport are an option – for the French regions Airport Transfer Services are good – www.a-t-s.net. Car hire is also reasonable from the airports, especially if booked beforehand on the internet. Once at the destination area a car is not essential, but very useful for many of the walks. Where available public transport is mentioned in the walks, but relying on it can be limiting, and not all small alpine villages are served by regular services. If you do hire a car be sure that it comes with snow chains or snow tyres, and a motorway sticker (*vignette*) if you are in Switzerland.

By Rail: Renowned for its TGV (Trains à Grande Vitesse), France has an efficient rail network. This now links to the Eurostar service which comes from Britain through the Channel Tunnel. Many of the small alpine towns are served by local train services.

In Switzerland the train service runs like clockwork, so don't expect to catch a train if you're a minute late

– it will have left. The trains often operate in conjunction with the Postbus system, which serves all villages with post offices throughout Switzerland.

The Italian trains and buses are a little more flexible, and the bus services in the alpine valleys are both reliable and an interesting social experience in high season.

By Road: The Alps are served by motorways which allow fast travel. French and Italian motorways have tolls, which are usually payable by credit card, but occasionally this is not possible in Italy. In Switzerland you must buy a sticker (*vignette*) to travel on the motorways, which lasts until the end of December each year.

In the winter you may well need snow chains on the higher roads in the Alps, and the passes above about 1800m are usually closed. You can ask the local tourist office or police for details.

WHEN TO GO

Some years the snow comes in November, other years not until January. It always comes eventually and if you can be very flexible then you can choose your time between November and late April by calling the local tourist office or searching the internet for snow conditions.

Solitude near Chamonix – returning from the Aiguillette des Houches (Route 22)

For those who have to plan ahead, January to April is usually the best time for snowshoeing in the Alps. Christmas can be excellent, but in the past decade there have been a few years when the deep snow-cover did not come until January.

In December and January the days are short, and usually quite cold but sunny. This means the snow stays cold, and is often light and a pleasure to walk in. Forests are magical with the trees blanketed in snow, and at this time of year it is possible to do walks at lower altitudes which will not retain snow later in the season.

February is the month of holidays, so there are lots of people in the towns and villages. Usually there's plenty of snow. March sees the days getting longer, but there is still lots of snow down to the valleys, except in the very low resorts. April can be anything from very sunny with fantastic stable snow conditions (but with the downside of ice and hard slopes in the morning) to fresh snow every day, as has happened some years lately. Any time after the first or second week of April is risky for snow conditions, and in the lower resorts the end of March is really the end of the snowshoe season.

It is important to consider the general aspect of the walk you are planning to do in relation to likely snow conditions. Not only is this essential when considering the avalanche risk but also, later in the season, it will maximize your chances of

29

Shadows on the snow

walking in suitable snow-cover. For example, even in late April there will usually be good snow on north- and west-facing slopes above 2000m, whereas the south faces may be snow-free up to 2500m.

The holiday seasons are: Christmas and New Year, most if not all of February, and Easter. January is probably the quietest time in most alpine regions. Hotel costs can vary during the season, with reductions outside the holiday times.

WHERE TO GO

An ideal snowshoe walk starts in a valley and makes its way up through forest, emerging above the treeline into an alpage from where there are wonderful views of the glaciated peaks nearby. There may be a beautiful old wooden chalet with a sunny balcony where you can enjoy your picnic before continuing up gentle

slopes to the summit. The descent is down slightly steeper slopes of deep powder, where you can run down in leaps and bounds before re-entering the forest and enjoying a final peaceful hour or so back to the valley.

There are many possibilities on snowshoes, but a certain amount of imagination is required to find new walks. It's a mistake to think that you can come to the Alps in winter and repeat trails that you've walked the previous summer. Winter and summer itineraries are often quite different – snow covers the paths, waymarks are usually hidden, traversing paths are often impassable or cross dangerous avalanche-prone slopes, and walks near ski resorts have become ski pistes.

The optimum altitude attained on snowshoe walks depends on the snow-cover. Early in the season snow levels would normally be expected to be low, around 800–1000m, so summits of 1800–2000m would be very good objectives. Later, as the snow level rises, you can hope to reach 2500–3000m and more. In addition to summits, the alpages themselves are also good objectives for a day's walk, as are cols. In bad weather it's often best to stay in the forests where you can see, as above the treeline visibility may be severely reduced.

To find snowshoe possibilities look on the 1:25,000 map for lower-altitude rounded summits which seem to be accessible without crossing rocky barriers or excessively steep slopes. Avoid peaks which depend on a traverse, especially where this is above steep slopes or a precipice. You will be surprised what gives a good day out in the winter.

BASES FOR A SNOWSHOE WALKING HOLIDAY

The walks in the guide are grouped by region, each region being centred on a major town. Some of these towns make good places to stay; others are a bit too industrialised and at low altitude. Each region described in the book has a list of suggested bases. However, this list is far from definitive – if another village or town takes your fancy, contact the local tourist office. Most offices have web sites, and if not the office in the nearest big town will be able to give you details. English is always spoken to some degree at tourist offices.

When deciding on your base, take into consideration the walks you hope to do, how far you wish to drive each day or if you're going to use public transport, the facilities you want to have available, and so on.

ALPINE ACCOMMODATION

All alpine resorts have **hotels** of varying standards, rated with a star system from no stars to 5 stars according to luxuriousness. Smaller villages will offer a more restricted range of accommodation, and will probably not have hotels at the upper end of the scale. In the smaller, traditional hotels it may be difficult to get single rooms in high season or to get en suite facilities.

The French towns and villages also have *gîtes d'étapes*, which provide dormitory accommodation and sometimes self-catering possibilities. Many Swiss alpine hotels and restaurants also have a dormitory tucked away under the eaves.

Alpine huts have varying opening times. Many are not open at all during the winter months. Others open for the ski-touring season (late March to mid-May), when the snow is usually at its most stable and the days are longer. Some only open for a part of this season. Many huts leave a small winter room open when the hut itself is closed. It will usually contain blankets, and sometimes a stove. A small number of huts stay open and wardened throughout the year.

A considerable number of huts are owned by the national alpine clubs, and details of these huts are

Synchronised descent

available from the clubs – the French, Swiss and Italian clubs have web sites. Private huts must be contacted direct. The French ones are all detailed in a useful book, *Guide Gîtes d'Etape et Refuges*, by Annick and Serge Mouraret, which is also found on www.gites-refuges.com. Many huts and *gîtes* also have web sites.

If you plan to do a snowshoe trek you need to plan carefully for accommodation. It may be difficult to do more than two or three days hut to hut, so you need to factor in some valley accommodation along the way. In high season it is essential to book in advance for both hut and hotel accommodation.

MOUNTAIN RESCUE IN THE ALPS

It is a sad fact, but accidents do happen in the mountains. By far the majority of winter accidents happen on the ski pistes, but with more and more people venturing into the hills in winter there has been a consequent increase in accidents there. Whilst zero risk doesn't exist in the Alps, especially in winter, your aim should be to reduce the dangers to an acceptable level – by using common sense and being properly informed and equipped for the terrain and conditions in which you plan to snowshoe. If you do have an accident in the European Alps, you will at least be relieved to know that usually help is fairly close at hand. The Alps are covered by a rescue service that is generally fast, efficient and well practised. Obviously there are occasional places that are less accessible, where you may have to wait longer for help, but in general you can expect to be receiving treatment soon after an accident.

It may appear that in the non-glaciated mountains the chances of needing rescuing are slight, but nevertheless the rescue services are regularly called out to incidents involving walkers in these areas. In addition to the general hazards of walking, such as fatigue, damaged ankles and knees, and head injuries from falls, there are the added winter complications of short, often cold days and variable snow conditions. Typical winter incidents (apart from skiing injuries) are cold injuries (frostbite and hypothermia), slips on icy slopes and avalanche injuries, either the result of burial or falls caused by the snowpack sliding. Snowshoeing on glaciated terrain carries the same risks, with the additional hazard of crevasses and icy ground in general. Roping up for glacier travel is not in itself a guarantee against falling into a gaping void. Using a rope badly is probably as dangerous as not using one at all, and every year the rescue services see lots of accidents on glaciers involving one or more members of a party that have fallen into a crevasse. Injuries can be very severe in these cases, including damaged limbs, torso and head, as well as hypothermia caused by a prolonged period in the ice.

Throughout the Alps rescues are carried out by professional bodies: in the Haute Savoie and Savoie regions of France near Mont Blanc the rescue organisation is the Peleton de Gendarmerie de la Haute Montagne (PGHM). In Italy rescues are carried out by Mountain Guides, employed on a rota basis, whilst the Swiss are served by private companies in different regions, using guides and other trained personnel as necessary.

So, what to do if the unthinkable happens and you need help in the mountains? Hopefully, you will be able to get down to the valley with the help of your group, but if this isn't the case you need to call the rescue services. The rapid development of mobile phones over the last few years has made this a much more viable option, even if the rescue service finds itself called out for a considerable number of trivial incidents. You must, however, know where you are and be coherent about your position and your condition. If possible give a grid reference (using the Swiss maps you will need to give an eight-figure reference, as each grid line is already three digits). You must also know your own phone number, as the rescue co-ordinator will want to call you back. If the weather is good, a helicopter will generally be sent to locate you as soon as possible. In bad weather, or if your situation is very difficult to access, you could be in for a wait, when your first-aid and survival knowledge and supplies may prove to be essential.

Although 112 is becoming a universally accepted emergency number, it's worth programming into your phone the number of the local rescue service. In the Chamonix area the number for the PGHM is 04 50 53 16 89. Not all countries use 112 regularly. In Switzerland the rescue number is 117, or 1414 for the REGA

rescue helicopter; in Italy 118 is the accepted number at the moment.

If you don't have a phone you may be able to find a passing walker or skier who has, but in this book some walks have been chosen specifically chosen for their solitude. In such cases, the nearest open mountain hut or ski lift station or village will be able to help, but be sure to pinpoint your victim's position on the map first and to make sure he is well protected from the cold or further injury. You should always insulate the casualty well – if you have ten pieces of clothing available, put nine underneath the victim and one on top.

When you hear the approaching helicopter, there are certain procedures to follow if you don't want to see your salvation heading off into the distance or, worse, to create more damage by doing something dangerous. You should have already prepared yourself for the helicopter's arrival by making your position obvious (using colourful clothing or getting out an orange bivvy bag, for example). The helicopter will generate a lot of wind and will blow the snow around, so gear and people should be firmly attached to the ground. There are accepted signals for indicating to the helicopter pilot that you need help. Put both arms in the air in a V to signal 'Yes, I need help', or put one arm up and one down to indicate 'No, I don't need help'.

If the accident has taken place on a slope, it will be easier for the rescue

services if you can move the casualty to an area of flat ground or a small knoll, free of trees. If this is not possible, then the person signalling to the helicopter should at least try to direct the helicopter to land in an area like this. This will make things much easier for the pilot, for whom it can be difficult to distinguish the angle of slopes in snowy terrain.

After this, let the rescue personnel organise everything. Many rescuers in the Alps speak English, so communication shouldn't be a problem. You'll soon be winging your way to the nearest hospital. In most sectors of the Alps the time-scale from calling out the rescue to arriving at the hospital will be less than an hour, although on very busy days, if you have a minor injury, you may have to wait longer. Clearly all this can change significantly if you have an accident alone, or in an isolated area, or if you don't have the means to call for help. In bad weather it may be possible to send up a rescue team on foot, but heavy snow can hinder these efforts, so going out when the forecast is bad significantly increases your risks in a rescue situation.

This is all very reassuring, but what about paying for your emergency services? Helicopters cost a lot of money, and the last thing you want to be thinking about when you've hurt yourself is whether you can afford to be rescued and treated. In France rescue is free, but any medical costs that ensue are not, nor is the cost of repatriation. Moreover, you will often be walking near and over national boundaries, and in Italy and Switzerland you can expect to pay for the rescue as well as all the subsequent treatment.

Insurance is widely available, and should be taken out to cover rescue on the terrain on which you plan to walk, and also to cover medical costs incurred and repatriation, should this be necessary.

THE WEATHER

Traditionally known as La Mauvaise Saison, in the past winter was a time to be survived, not enjoyed. Winter was a time of recuperation after the toils of summer, La Belle Saison, but also a time of hardship, especially if the har-

vests hadn't been good or if the snow was unusually heavy or prolonged.

Now winter sees as many visitors to the Alps as summer, many of them there for the snow – the 'white gold' as it is sometimes known.

Whilst the weather can certainly be unpredictable, there are nevertheless some general patterns that can be described. The mountains are of course affected by general European weather systems, but they also create their own localised anomalies. As a frontal system approaches the Alps the air, laden with moisture from the sea, it has to rise over the mountains, resulting in a cooling of the air, turning water vapour into droplets and consequently precipitation. The precipitation sometimes falls mainly on

High winds on the Col Serena (Route 58) (photo: Jon de Montjoye)

WEATHER AND AVALANCHE INFORMATION

By Phone
France
Weather 08 92 68 02 + Department number eg. 74 for Chamonix
Avalanche 08 92 68 10 20 + * Department number when told to.

Switzerland
Weather: 162 Press 1 when told to then # (diaz) when told to.
Avalanche 187

Italy (Aosta region)
Weather: 0165 44113
Avalanche: 0165 776300
No forecast is regularly available by phone in English at present.

On the Web
French Alps
www.meteofrance.com. This also provides three-day forecasts for Europe
and the world.

Swiss Alps
www.tsr.ch/meteo/meteo.html Swiss Romande tv forecast: general and
simple.
www.sfdrs.ch/sendungen/meteo/ Swiss German tv forecast
www.wsl.ch/slf/laworg/map.html Swiss Federal Institute for Snow and
Avalanche Research. Good site for Europe, includes avalanche forecasts and
weather forecasts, and can be had in English.

Italian Alps
www.regione.vda.it Weather and avalanche forecasts.
www.cai-svi.it Italian Alpine Club site, with mountain weather and avalanche reports.
www. aineva.it The Interregional Snow and Avalanche Association. Good
site for Italian snow conditions and forecasts.

General sites
www.csac. org Cyber Space Avalanche Centre.
www.chamonix.com General information and weather reports.
www.zermatt.com General information.
www.sac-cas.ch The Swiss Alpine Club site provides lots of useful links.

one side of a range of peaks, leaving the other in a rain shadow, enjoying relatively dry conditions. This classically happens in the Mont Blanc massif when, for example the weather

example a westerly front is often accompanied by a southerly foehn, and frequently the wind changes direction after a front has passed. So if it's snowing in Chamonix there's a

When the massif looks like this it is probably best to plan a valley walk

can come from the south, giving heavy rain or snow on the Italian side of the range whilst the Chamonix valley is protected and basks in the sun. The opposite is sometimes true when the weather comes from the north. This effect is caused by a 'foehn' wind – a southern foehn causes rain on the Italian side of the Alps, while a northern foehn means that Italy will be largely dry, whilst France and parts of Switzerland get the bad weather.

A front can be accompanied by winds from a different direction, for

chance it will be sunny in Courmayeur and vice versa.

Mountain weather can change very suddenly, so you must always get a weather forecast before heading out. These are available at local tourist offices, guide's bureaux, and by phone or internet. However, don't base your plan too rigidly on what is predicted – sometimes fronts come in more quickly or more slowly than anticipated (maybe by up to 6 hours), an anticyclone can hold off a front for longer than expected, or a very localised change can affect the out-come. Look at the sky, and if you can see the weather worsening rethink your plans for that day. Classic signs include thin wispy clouds caused by high winds at altitude; increasing wind in the valleys; cumulus clouds build-ing in the mountains; and locals carry-ing umbrellas.

Forecasts are generally put out in the local language – a brief glossary of terms is given at the back of this book – but you can always ask at the local tourist offices, where somebody will speak English. One vitally important piece of information in winter is the altitude at which the temperature reaches 0°C, as this will give an idea of the state and stability of the snow.

GRADES OF WALKS

It is extremely difficult to grade snow-shoe walks since there are so many variables, not least the state of the snow. As a general guide, the walks in this book have been graded on a scale of 1–4, 4 being the most difficult. Glacier walks are graded G4 or G5 (see below).

The following criteria have been taken into account:
- altitude gain
- length of the walk, especially when the height gain is relatively modest
- steepness of the slopes
- objective dangers (navigation dif-ficulties, route finding, avalanche risks, etc)
- technical sections

- remoteness of the area
- whether the walk takes place on a glacier, in which case the high-est grade, preceded by a G, is

GRADING SCALE

Grade 1: An easy walk, usually half a day, with no steep slopes or associated difficulties.

Grade 2: A full-day walk, some-times quite long with a certain amount of height gain, but few if any technical sections.

Grade 3: These walks will certainly include some steeper slopes, maybe some traverses, route-find-ing and considerable height gain.

Grade 4: Walks graded 4 on non-glaciated terrain are at the limit of what can be done on snowshoes, and for such walks you should go equipped with crampons and be prepared to take off your snow-shoes for steeper sections. These walks will be long and arduous.

Grade G4: Any glacier walk is given at least this grade as the walk requires you to have knowledge of safe glacier travel (see 'Glacier Travel', p.58).

Grade G5: this denotes long and arduous glacier walks where not only is there a lot of climbing and ground to be covered but there is also a considerable potential for difficult navigation or hazardous slopes.

given regardless of actual technical difficulty; technical glacier walks then get a higher grade still.

Inevitably some walks overlap two categories, and these have been given a grade such as 2/3. It is essential to understand that the grading of a walk is based on its usual condition. However, snow or weather conditions can quickly change a grade 1 walk into a grade 2; fog, deep snow, high winds – all these factors make a huge difference. You must adapt your choice of walk according to the conditions and be prepared to turn back before the walk becomes more serious than you are able to cope with.

TIMINGS

In the same way that it is difficult to grade a walk, it is also hard to assign to each walk a suggested time, as in winter there are so many variables that can affect the time needed for a walk.

Timings are included purely as a guide, and in no way as a spur to performance, and they can be nothing more than an approximation. The times have been calculated on the accepted alpine assumption that the average walker climbs about 300m per hour on snowshoes and descends at a rate of 500m. This calculation works fine in the Alps for any slopes, be they steep or gentle. There is no need to factor in a time for the distance, as this is taken into account by

Fresh snow, good weather, great walk – on the Pointe d'Arpille (Route 45) (photo: Jon de Montjoye)

the steepness of the slope. Only where there are long flat sections should you then calculate progress at about 3km per hour.

Such times are affected noticeably by snow conditions (heavy fresh snowfall), steep slopes, stream beds, rocky ground, and so on, when progression becomes much more difficult and you should adjust your time accordingly, being ready to shorten the walk if necessary.

The times given allow you to enjoy the scenery, take the time to study animal tracks and generally enjoy the experience. If you find they don't suit you, then calculate your own times and adapt accordingly. Remember that the times in the book do not include lunch breaks or any other lengthy stops. However, it is important for those coming from Britain, where Naismith's rule for calculating walking time is generally accepted, to understand that in the Alps you cannot calculate times with anything like this precision. Hence the timings given for the walks here are generous and very approximate.

In the Alps it is important to pace yourself for the walk, avoiding fast starts or irregular speeds, which can leave you exhausted for the rest of the outing. A slow, rhythmic plod is by far the most effective and pleasant way to reach the top and still have the energy to descend.

DIRECTIONS

Directions are given in the route descriptions on the assumption that readers have a map in front of them. Where left and right are used, these refer to the direction that the walker is going (according to the route description) and will often be qualified with a compass direction. When referring to rivers and glaciers the use of the terms 'true right bank' and 'true left bank' assumes the walker is looking down the flow.

ROUTE DESCRIPTIONS AND SKETCH MAPS

The route descriptions indicate the main landmarks and places where a change of direction is necessary. Often other features, such as the terrain and the angle of the slope encountered, are also described.

In the route description mention is often made of paths and tracks which will be more or less snow covered, depending on conditions. However, even in deep snow it is often possible to make out the vague outline of these paths, especially in forests. They are referred to only in such locations.

The parking areas at the start of walks are sometimes small, and although these are the established starting points for the walks in winter, in exceptional conditions they may not be snow-free. In such cases it may be necessary to park further away, and consequently the extra walking time must be factored in to the total

Picking a line between seracs and crevasses

walk time. Please do not park in areas which have obviously been dug out by residents for their own cars.

The route descriptions are intended to complement the sketch maps, which must be used in conjunction with the 1:25,000 or 1:50,000 map of the area. The refuge symbol on the sketch maps indicates refuges designated in the route description as an overnight stop.

ASPECT

The principal aspect of each walk is given. This is important in the winter when, for example, strong winds may have deposited slab on certain slopes or warm conditions may mean that

The end of the day at the Bec Rond (Route 32) –
shady slopes can give powder descents, but beware of avalanche risk

there is a lack of snow on south-facing slopes.

MAPS

It is essential that you have the appropriate map for the walk you are planning to do. The sketch maps in this guide are just to show the route, but do not in any way replace the full maps. Whether you choose the 1:25,000 or 1:50,000 is really a matter of personal preference. Where possible, references in the text are consistent with the maps produced in the country that the walk is located in. There will often be other maps available for the same area. For the 1:50,000 Swiss maps it is recommend that you get the ski versions if available – these have the same reference number but it is preceded by an S. These show the lines of ski tours which will often take the same route as snowshoe routes. This means that you are not distracted by the summer paths shown in red on the summer versions.

Some maps do change a lot when they are updated. The text tries to indicate where names have been changed, but this will not be definitive. Sometimes place names vary slightly in their spelling from one map to another – where this difference is important it is noted.

The new French 1:25,000 maps are GPS friendly – this means that they have grid lines and references on them. The Swiss maps also give this information, but the Italian ones – well, I'll leave you to discover the joys of Italian maps! Suffice to say, they can be a little vague.

It should be noted that some mountain areas of Switzerland are used by the military for training. At these times the areas are closed to the public. Details of closures are posted on signs locally.

GUIDED SNOWSHOEING

You may judge that you don't yet have the skills to snowshoe independently. There are lots of companies offering snowshoe holidays, and in all alpine resorts you'll find guided snowshoeing trips available. Many of them will be very low level, designed for the beginner who just fancies a try. The gear provided will be adequate for the walk proposed, but will probably not be high quality and may give a poor impression for the first-timer. However, such walks do give an initial experience of snowshoeing, and most will be led by a local who is probably a mine of information about the region, animal tracks, traditional life, and so on.

Showshoers of any level of experience may decide they would like to benefit from the knowledge of a professional guide. You can ask at the local tourist offices for a guide to take you on hikes adapted to your level.

The only people qualified to lead commercial walks are:

- Accompagnateur en Montagne (France)
- Accompagnatore di Montagna (Italy)

The Tête de la Fonteinte provides perfect views

- Accompanador de Montana (Spain)
- Bergwanderfürher (Germany, Austria and German-speaking Switzerland)
- European Mountain Leader (Britain) – check that the person has been trained in snowshoeing.
- UIAGM High Mountain Guide.

For glaciated ground, only the UIAGM guide is legally able to guide. Ask to see proof of the qualification of anyone offering to guide walks, as an unqualified person, experienced though they may be, is not insured to lead paying clients. Switzerland has no law yet (2002) as regards non-glaciated terrain, but on glaciers a UIAGM guide's certificate is required.

LANGUAGES

The walks described in this book cover three language areas. French is spoken in France and in Switzerland from the French border to Lake Geneva to Sierre. Beyond Sierre, Swiss German is spoken. In Italy expect to hear Italian and French – the borders have changed in relatively recent times, and north of Aosta many people are fluent in French.

In fact part of the Swiss Canton of Valais, the Haute Savoie and the Valdotain were all part of the Kingdom of Savoy at one time, and consequently share similar old dialects.

SAFETY AND TECHNICAL INFORMATION

As with all outdoor activities things can go wrong when snowshoeing, and these problems can be aggravated by the cold.

HAZARDS OF THE EQUIPMENT

Despite the manufacturer's best intentions, snowshoes do sometimes break, and you need to be prepared for this. No shoe is perfect, and it is important to check your equipment for any signs of wear and tear before going out. Carry a small repair kit (see 'Snowshoe Equipment', p.56).

HAZARDS ON THE TRAIL

As beautiful as they are, mountains and forests can be unforgiving in winter. With a good imagination you can probably dream up lots of potential dangers; here are just two.

Losing your way: Above the treeline, and often also in the forest, it is not usually possible to distinguish the route of summer paths and trails, so you'll have to navigate by the lie of the land, using your compass and looking at the map. Do not rely on snowshoe tracks to guide you, unless you are

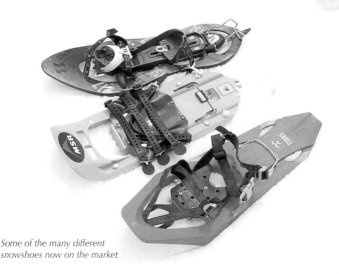

Some of the many different snowshoes now on the market

No weather hazards in these conditions in the Aravis (Route 9)

very familiar with the area in winter and summer, as you can't be sure where these tracks are going, and any change in the weather could mean the track is quickly obliterated. The same warning applies to the notion of retracing your steps – you'd be surprised how fast your own track is totally lost in fog or fresh snow. Make sure you always know where you are. A Global Positioning System can be very useful so long as you are experienced in using it, but there's really nothing in mountain navigation that you can't do with a map and compass.

Falling into water: Under cover of snow, lakes and streams can be difficult to discern. Whilst in summer conditions slipping into a stream may be more amusing than dangerous, it is a different story in winter, when you'll very quickly become seriously cold. Stream crossings can also be delicate and potentially life-threatening. Snow bridges can collapse, and the snowshoer can fall through to be washed downstream under snow-cover. Similarly, falling into a frozen lake can lead to drowning when the victim is caught under ice.

WEATHER HAZARDS

Inaccurate forecasts: With the best will in the world forecasters can only work with the information available, and sometimes they are proved wrong. Snowshoers have to able to cope if the weather deteriorates. Be

ready to alter your plans according to changes in the weather, and you will need to be able to navigate if the fog comes in or a blizzard blows up.

Lapse rate and wind chill: It may be a comfortable 12°C in the valley, but as you gain altitude it becomes colder. This is known as the lapse rate. Technically the temperature drops by .65°C for every 100m of ascent. However, the lapse rate can be affected by temperature inversions and also by the humidity in the air. Temperatures drop noticeably in the shade, at night and during storms. The wind also dramatically affects the temperature, and the combined cooling effect of wind plus air temperature is known as wind chill. This is particularly important in winter. For any given air temperature the cooling effect (wind-chill factor) increases rapidly with increasing wind speed. For example, with an air temperature of 0°C and wind speed of 40km/h the temperature will feel like -13°C; at -5°C with wind speed of 15km/h it will feel like -11°C; at -15°C with wind speed 20km/h it will feel like -26°C.

MEDICAL HAZARDS

There are several medical situations that are more common in winter.

Hypothermia: Sometimes referred to as exposure, hypothermia occurs when the body starts to lose heat faster than it can produce it, and consequently the body's core temperature, that of the trunk of the body, drops. This situation is potentially very dangerous, and it is important to recognise the problem before it becomes life-threatening.

First signs are shivering, fatigue and clumsiness. Next the shivering will intensify, and the victim will have difficulty speaking and performing normal tasks. If not treated at this stage (mild hypothermia) the situation will become much more serious. A profoundly hypothermic victim will stop shivering, and his mental ability will deteriorate to the extent that he may believe he's hot and try to remove clothing or become aggressive. As core temperature continues to drop the muscles become rigid, and pulse and respiration slow. Death can occur when the temperature drops below 30°C, and death regularly occurs at 20°C.

A hypothermic victim should be sheltered from the wind, and extra layers of insulation added. A victim should have his wet clothing removed and replaced by dry clothing only if the hypothermia is mild or intermediate and if he is not exposed to cold when undressed. **Mildly hypothermic** victims should be given warm drinks and food, and warmed using external heat sources such as hot water bottles or heaters. They should not continue with the walk – they should take the quickest and easiest way back.

A **profoundly hypothermic** person is in, or on the verge of, a coma,

and their already very delicate state can easily be aggravated by incorrect care. Nothing should be administered by mouth. Instead all efforts should be made to prevent further heat loss, whilst handling the victim very carefully. The heart is extremely sensitive to the cold, and abrupt movement can cause ventricular fibrillation. Rewarming a profoundly hypothermic victim is best done in a hospital in controlled conditions. The victim requires rescue.

Frostbite: Frostbite is surprisingly common in the Alps and can be very serious. It develops when tissue is exposed to sub-freezing cold and can be divided into three stages.

- *Frostnip or first degree frostbite.* This is the body's first response to freezing temperatures and involves stinging pain, numbness and white skin. It often occurs on the cheeks, ears, nose or fingertips.
- *Superficial or second degree frostbite.* This will happen if the first stage is ignored. The skin becomes pale or grey and cold to the touch. Blisters will form a day or so later, and the affected area will be very sore for some time.
- *Deep second or third degree frostbite.* Here you're in serious trouble as this is the deep freezing of the tissues. The injured area is grey or blue-black, cool to

the touch and void of sensation. Blisters will form, and the area will swell. When the tissue dies and turns black this is defined as third degree, and these parts will probably fall off or have to be amputated after a few weeks.

Frostnip should be treated as soon as you notice it by warming the affected area – putting hands in armpits for example, wrapping your face with a scarf. Second and third degree frostbite, however, are more difficult to treat. Treatment should take place inside when there's no chance that the thawed part will be refrozen. The key to recovery from frostbite is rapid rewarming, usually in warm water (40–42°C). This should take about 30 minutes.

The best way to beat frostbite is to avoid it in the first place.
- Eat well before and during a trip and take along a hot drink.
- Avoid tight clothing and boots.
- Cover up vulnerable areas such as neck and face as soon as you feel cold.
- Never touch metal with bare hands in sub-freezing temperatures.
- Be able to put on and take off your snowshoes and your rucksack without removing your gloves.
- If you start to get really cold, change your itinerary and take a shorter route or one that is at

lower altitude or more sheltered. Never be afraid to turn back.

Sunburn: This may seem to be more of a summer problem, but how often have you had sunburn under your arms on the beach? Remember, in snowy conditions the sun is reflecting up from the snow as well as down from the sky. Suncream should be applied under your arms as well as on the upper parts, under your nose and chin, on the back of your hands, and anywhere else that's exposed.

Snow-blindness: If your eyes are not adequately protected, the sun's rays can burn the surface of the eyes causing snow-blindness. Symptoms don't develop until several hours after exposure. Then you'll feel like your eyes are full of sand. In more severe cases this dryness and irritability causes difficulty seeing and severe pain. To prevent this, sunglasses must be worn, or goggles if visibility is bad.

HAZARDS OF THE SNOW

If you snowshoe anywhere other than on flat terrain with no steep slopes above, you must learn about avalanche awareness. This can only in part be learnt from books (see bibliography, p.279), and there is no replacement for practical experience on a specialised course or with an expert in the field. By recognising the avalanche danger and by gaining knowledge and experience, the risk can be greatly reduced.

It seems like the perfect day, but the avalanche warning flag tells a different story

Avalanches are the result of several factors:
- the amount of snow
- recent weather conditions
- current temperature
- previous conditions which have formed the snowpack
- activity on the snow slope.

Most winter recreationalists involved in an avalanche accident have triggered the avalanche themselves due to the extra loading on the slope. A weak layer in the snowpack may collapse, or a poor bond between two layers may fail, which can propagate to release a large slab. With irregular and thin (less than 1m) snowpack this danger is extremely difficult to recognise. The extra loading is more likely to collapse a weak layer, especially as a weak layer of loose sugary crystals

can often be found just above the ground at the base of the snowpack.

By careful route-finding and good group organisation the risk is greatly reduced. Keep off slopes of over 30° where possible and avoid terrain traps (narrow valleys, streambeds, slopes above cliffs/trees). Remember that even on flat ground it is possible to release a slab from above. By good spacing between group members when in potentially dangerous zones you are less likely to trigger an avalanche, and can quickly implement a self-rescue if someone is caught.

Shady (northerly) slopes tend to keep their instabilities longer than those warmed by the sun's rays. With increased temperatures the snow undergoes considerable transformation. As a rule the risk of avalanches increases with the time of day, especially in the spring. This can go from **low** (in early morning after a clear night) to **considerable** in the afternoon.

A sudden rise in temperature with strong sun, warm wind or rain increases the avalanche risk. Subsequent cooling on the other hand has a stabilising effect.

The risk of avalanches rises abruptly with fresh snowfall and windy, cold conditions. Drifting snow quickly accumulates on lee slopes causing massive differences in snow depths, particularly noticeable on slopes exposed to cross-winds. This drifting can continue to occur during clear but windy weather. **The first fine day after a storm is particularly dangerous.** 10–20cm of fresh snow with wind is enough to create a critical situation. Slopes near ridges and cols are frequently dangerous.

Take note of the local avalanche bulletin and advice of local experts. Look out for any activity identifying avalanche start zones, their tracks and run-out zones – in particular any 'whumping' noises or shooting cracks when walking. This is a sure sign of instability, as a less dense layer in the snowpack is collapsing. Be aware too of the possible effect of this collapse, which can propagate into steeper terrain, especially if this is above you.
   If in doubt stay off the slope.

Avalanche Risk Scale: In Europe and America the scale on p.52 is used to rate the avalanche risk daily during the winter. However this is only for guidance, and each slope should be regarded as unique.

   Avalanche risk predictions can be found in ski resorts, at tourist offices and guide's offices. Often they do not use the risk level number, just the description; the description is therefore included below in French, German and Italian. (Note: Zero risk level doesn't exist.)

Avalanche beacons: If you are snowshoeing anywhere except flat terrain with no steep slopes above, you should be equipped with an avalanche beacon and know how to use it. This should be attached to your body, next to your base layer of clothing, and it should be turned on to transmit mode.

   Beacons work by emitting a signal that can be picked up by other beacons set to the receive mode. If someone wearing a functioning beacon is buried in an avalanche he can be searched for and usually found very quickly. This is vital, as the chance of surviving an avalanche is greatest (93%) in the first 15 minutes after burial, whereas after 30 minutes the likelihood of a live recovery drops to 50%.

   All modern beacons operate on the same frequency, 457kHz, so there should be no problems of compatibility. Instructions for use are supplied with beacons, and you need to learn

AVALANCHE RISK SCALE

Level 1 *Low, faible, gering, debole*. Natural avalanches are very unlikely, and human-triggered avalanches unlikely. The snowpack is well consolidated on the majority of slopes. Avalanches are possible only by heavy loading on isolated steep slopes. Travel is generally safe, normal caution advised.

Level 2 *Moderate, limité, mässig, moderato*. Natural avalanches unlikely; human-triggered avalanches possible. On some steep slopes the snowpack is not completely consolidated, and heavy loading could produce an avalanche.

Level 3 *Considerable, marqué, erheblich, marcato*. Natural avalanches possible; human-triggered avalanches probable. On numerous slopes the snowpack is not consolidated, and avalanches can be set off by even light loading of some slopes.

Level 4 *High, fort, gross, forte*. Natural and human-triggered avalanches likely, as the snowpack is not consolidated on most slopes. Avalanches can be expected by light loading of slopes. Safest travel on windward ridges or lower-angle slopes without steeper terrain above.

Level 5 *Very high, très fort, sehr gross, molto forte*. Very high risk of avalanche. Widespread natural and human-triggered avalanches certain. The snowpack is unconsolidated on all slopes. Many large spontaneous avalanches are likely even on relatively gentle-angled slopes, and lines of communication are threatened. Travel of any kind should be avoided.

to use yours and then practise regularly finding buried beacons.

Shovel and probe: These are vital pieces of equipment. Without a shovel it is extremely difficult to excavate someone from an avalanche, and a probe enables you to search for a deeply buried victim.

How to avoid an avalanche and what to do if you don't: Certain tips are given below on avalanche avoidance, but in the end experience and caution are the key factors.
• Treat all slopes as guilty until proved innocent. Most avalanches occur on slopes of 30–45°, but even slopes of 20° and

US AND EUROPEAN AVALANCHE WARNINGS

In Europe the following flags will be flying at ski resorts and alpine villages.

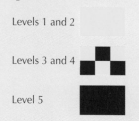

Levels 1 and 2

Levels 3 and 4

Level 5

If the black flag is flying don't even think of going snowshoeing. Stay home and do something sensible!

In America and Canada the colours of the risk scale are:

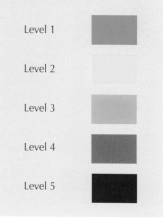

Level 1

Level 2

Level 3

Level 4

Level 5

less have been seen to avalanche. Pick your route carefully, staying away from steep slopes and avoiding places where an avalanche from above would be inescapable. Where there is an option, try to keep to crests and ridges rather that traversing suspect slopes.

- Don't stop for lunch or a rest in any area that might be a run-out zone for an avalanche slope or gully.
- If you must cross a suspect slope, go one person at a time, the others staying in a safe place (sheltered beneath a boulder for example or well off the slope), all watching carefully as each person crosses.
- Don't go near cornices – on top or underneath.
- If you need to ascend or descend a slope try to do so in an area of dense forest – a few trees won't prevent an avalanche.

If caught in an avalanche, you are advised to do the following.
- In the split second before you're carried down try to jump above the fracture line or out to the side.
- Shout to alert others.
- Then keep your mouth shut so as not to let it fill with snow.
- Drop your poles.
- Try to stay on the surface of the avalanche by making swimming motions.

- When you feel the snow coming to a stop, try to make an air pocket in front of your face with your hand.

Snowshoeing is a serious business but it can be done safely, and in all but the most dangerous conditions there's usually somewhere you can go for a walk, even if it's just around the local golf course – in bad weather this is probably a great outing.

To go out and come back safely in the Alps you must be experienced in navigation, avalanche awareness, and survival in the cold, and you must, most importantly, know when to turn back. If you don't have these skills then hire someone who does to take you (see 'Guided Showshoeing', p.43).

Fully equipped for snow-shoeing, with beacon attached securely to the body

SNOWSHOE CLOTHING

What you wear when snowshoeing is largely a question of personal preference, but bear in mind that you'll usually experience a wide range of temperatures during the day, from the early morning cold, to the sweaty heat of the sunny midday ascent, to the cool of the descent from the summit. Add to that the fact that any precipitation will probably fall as snow, and you need to be well prepared.

No special clothing is needed, just normal hiking gear, but plenty of it. Padded ski apparel should be avoided, as it is usually too hot and bulky when you're exerting yourself.

As in all mountain activities, the layering principle works best: a thermal layer next to the skin, which wicks moisture away, a second fleece or wool layer for warmth and finally a more or less waterproof breathable layer on top to keep out wind, snow or worse. Obviously extra layers can be added as desired, but, whatever you do, leave the cotton T-shirts at home – cotton clothing can be deadly, as it absorbs moisture easily and loses all insulating value when wet.

A hat is vital in winter: the body loses a large proportion of heat through the head, hence the saying 'If your feet are cold put on a hat'. Gloves are essential: ski gloves work fine, as do thick wool, fleece or leather. If you suffer from cold fingers, mittens are more effective at keeping your hands warm.

Gaiters keep the snow out of your boots. Ankle length are often adequate, but full knee length ones are better in deep snow, even if they are rather hot in sunny conditions.

Good sunglasses are required for snow travel as the snow reflects light, and insufficient protection can cause snow blindness. In bad visibility you'll find yellow-tinted goggles give you more defined vision. Goggles are also useful in blizzards when snowflakes blow into your eyes.

SNOWSHOE EQUIPMENT

So you've got your snowshoes, what else do you need?

Poles: For me there is no question – poles are not an option, they are essential for any snowshoe outing (except snowshoe running) at whatever level of difficulty. However, my opinion is not shared by everyone, and you will almost certainly see snowshoers without poles and read in some books that they are not essential. Reasons for my opinion are given below, but the decision is yours.

- Poles give stability in all conditions and on all terrain; this is most obvious when you're making the trail in deep snow, but is equally true when you're strolling on a flat prepared trail. Without, you are ungainly.
- It is far more tiring to snowshoe without poles, as all your weight is on your legs and back.
- Poles help to spread the load,

and pushing with your arms serves to help propel you forward.
- Poles are extremely useful when ascending, to keep you upright, and also for descending, for the same reason. They are equally important for clearing snow-laden branches that may block your way.

The type of poles doesn't really matter – telescopic or not, trekking poles, ski sticks, – but the round basket on the bottom should be reasonably large, not the small trekking variety, as this stops the pole disappearing up to your armpit in the snow

Your poles should become extensions of your arms, if you are lucky

Boots: Certain criteria should be taken into account when choosing boots for snowshoeing.

- Boots must be waterproof and warm in winter conditions. Leather or plastic, it doesn't really matter, but your boots must provide at least adequate protection from the elements. In spring conditions three-season boots might suffice, but in the depths of winter you need four-season footwear.
- The sole should provide excellent traction on hard snow, and the heel must be vertical (not rounded down to the sole), otherwise you can't walk down snow safely.
- The ankle should be supportive.
- Your toes should not hit the end of the boots when walking downhill – this is very important as you often have to descend directly on snowshoes, without the subtle changes of position that are possible when descending on dry ground.
- Make sure the boots fit with the socks that you will be wearing for snowshoeing, which will probably be quite thick for warmth.
- Don't forget to check that your boots fit the bindings of the snowshoes (or vice versa, depending on which comes first).

Rucksack: The size of your pack is clearly dependent on the trips you plan to do. You must be able to get all

your gear inside the sac, including emergency items such as shovel and probe, and your warm clothing, which you'll often shed going uphill. Nothing should be hung on the outside of the sac, as this risks being lost when you fall in deep snow. However, it is advisable to keep the size of your sac within reasonable limits, as a huge sac is extremely tiring to carry, particularly when you also have the snow and the cold to contend with.

You need some way to attach your snowshoes to your sac so that you can carry them when necessary. Special snowshoe sacs exist, usually with an exterior flap to put over the shoes. Otherwise side-straps are effective, or you can put the shoes under the lid of the sac. Snowboard sacs can also be suitable for snowshoes.

Snowshoe repair kit: Depending on the type of snowshoes, different problems can occur, but most if not all can be temporarily repaired on the hill quite easily, allowing you to use them until you can have them mended properly. The most common problem is broken bindings. For these take duct tape, thin wire, cord or sturdy Velcro straps – anything that will enable you to keep your boot attached to the snowshoe. For bindings of the step-in crampon variety you should take a spare toe bail, as this can break, especially in very cold temperatures. Usually the manufacturers can supply spares. Snowshoes with soft decks can get torn, or the lacing of the deck to the frame can get worn. These parts should be frequently checked, but again duct tape will probably perform on-the-hill first aid. A penknife is always useful.

An ice-axe and crampons: You only need to take these if, firstly, you are experienced in their use and, secondly, you think there's a good chance that the terrain you encounter will require these tools. It is not usual on non-glaciated snowshoe walks to need an ice-axe, and carrying one doesn't ensure that you'll avoid a fall – you need to know how to self-arrest, and in those circumstances you probably shouldn't be wearing snowshoes. However, being able to cut steps with an axe could get you past a difficult slope more safely.

On glaciers an ice-axe should be carried, and glacier travel techniques need to be learnt from experienced people and practised regularly.

Avalanche equipment: This is covered in the section 'Hazards of the Snow', p.49. On anything other than flat terrain with no steep slopes above, the following equipment should be carried:
- avalanche beacon – worn next to the body and turned on, not carried in pack or pocket
- shovel
- probe.

First aid kit: This should be basic and not too heavy. If you are just going out

Emergency gear

for one day, plasters and pain killers should be enough. If you are going multi-day, then you need to be able to cope with stomach problems and other ailments that may arise.

Glacier travel equipment: This needs to be carried only if such terrain is to be encountered. When travelling on glaciers it is vital to be correctly equipped and to be well practised in crevasse rescue techniques (see 'Glacier Travel', p.58).

Normal emergency hillwalking gear: The following items should be taken when showshoeing:
- emergency blanket
- whistle
- phone (if you are in an area that has a network)
- spare food
- warm clothing

- map
- compass
- raingear
- sunscreen – minimum factor 15 – face and lips
- hat and gloves plus spare pair of gloves
- headtorch (can be a good idea as winter days are short)
- sunhat.

GLACIER TRAVEL AND CREVASSE RESCUE TECHNIQUES

Whilst there are plenty of non-glaciated summits to tackle on snow-shoes, you may eventually choose to go higher and experience the high mountain environment. This is the realm of glaciers, which introduce a whole new dimension into snowshoe-ing, notably that of the dangers of cre-vasses. With the right equipment and, far more importantly, with the right knowledge, these dangers can be reduced to an acceptable level. This knowledge can be gained in part from books, but there is really no substitute for experience – either going with experienced friends or by paying for professional instruction by qualified guides. **It is essential that you are experienced in glacier travel before venturing onto any of the glaciated walks in this book.**

The principal hazard of glacier travel is that of hidden crevasses. On a dry glacier (i.e. a glacier not covered with snow) crevasses are obvious and therefore pose no problems. However, on a wet (snow-covered) glacier what

58

lurks beneath the surface presents a very real danger.

Travel on a wet glacier is always undertaken roped together – even if there is a good track and good visibil-ity. Roping up wrongly and/or using the rope incorrectly can make any cre-vasse incident worse. It is therefore essential to adopt correct practice and to keep to certain guidelines.

This following information is not intended as an instruction manual for the novice, but as a reminder for those who already have these skills.

Glacier travel and crevasse rescue techniques must be learnt and prac-tised, either on a specialised course or from an experienced mountaineer or a professional.

Glacier travel and rescue proce-dures for a party of two people are described below. Each participant should be equipped with the mini-mum of an ice-axe, a harness and screwgate krab, an ice screw, a 120cm sling, three prussik loops, a pulley and three spare karabiners. The party should have a dynamic rope, the mini-mum diameter of which should be 8mm, though in practice a larger diameter is more user-friendly when it comes to handling in a crevasse-res-cue situation. It is not necessary to have a designated single rope of 10mm or 11mm if only pure glacier travel is envisaged. The minimum length should be about 30m for two people. For larger numbers a longer rope or two ropes should be used.

The walkers should be roped

together with about 10m of rope between them. To do this each should tie into the ends of the rope and take an equal number of coils around their shoulders until the middle 10m is left. The coils are tied off by passing a bight of rope around them and tying an overhand knot around the rope that leads between the walkers. This leaves a loop which can be clipped back into the harness with the screw-gate karabiner.

Walking on the glacier: When walking the rope should be kept reasonably tight – so that only the middle 5–6m glide along the snow (see Figure 1). If this tension is maintained, not only will the rope be kept away from sharp crampons but it also avoids the dangerous practice of walkers holding the rope up in their hand, which can result in a serious shoulder injury in the event of a crevasse fall.

One trekking pole should be stowed away on the rucksack leaving that hand free for the ice-axe. The axe **must** be instantly available for arresting a fall, not attached to the back of

the rucksack. It should be carried by the head, with the shaft downwards like a walking stick, in the uphill hand whenever appropriate.

Two further refinements of this basic system are the pre-attachment of prussik loops to the rope and the tying of knots in the rope at intervals along the 10m. The theory behind the latter method is that in the event of a crevasse fall the rope will cut into the snow lip and the knot will jam into the snow, thus arresting the fall. The downside of this system is that if the snow is very soft the knot will pass right through the snow and will hinder the consequent rescue.

It is worth considering putting the lightest person at the front, as disparity in weight is an important factor – if the lighter person falls in the crevasse the heavier person will find it easier to pull him out. But bear in mind that it is not always the first person to cross that breaks a fragile snowbridge.

Although both members of the party should be vigilant at all times on a glacier, some particularly crevassed areas will obviously be more dangerous than others. This information should be passed back from the leader so that the second person can prepare himself and tighten the rope further.

Arresting a fall: The first reaction to one of the walkers falling into a crevasse can determine success or

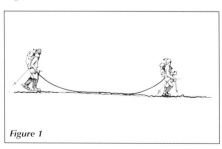

Figure 1

Figure 2

failure. If the other person is pulled flat on his face, then arresting the fall becomes very difficult. The ideal reaction is to jerk backwards and adopt a semi-sitting position, with the shaft of the axe plunged into the snow (see Figure 2). At this point it will be best to remove snowshoes to enable heels to kick in to provide a solid stance.

Before doing anything else the rescuer should do the following.

1   Shout to try to make contact with the victim – it may well be that by lowering him slightly he will be able to walk out of the crevasse on the other side.

2   Look around for other people – a group of 4–5 will be able to use brute force to pull the victim up or, at worst, help in the following stages of the rescue.

3   Ascertain whether it is possible

for the victim to ascend the rope using his prussik loops, assuming he knows how to do this.

Constructing a belay and transferring the victim's weight: The basic belay for crevasse rescue in snow is the horizontally buried ice-axe (see Figure 3). If the snow isn't deep enough then this is where the ice screw comes in. A slot must first be cut, using the axe, at right angles to the pull of the rope and as deep as possible. It should be the length of the axe and the forward wall should be slightly incut to avoid the axe being pulled out. A second slot, this time in line with the pull, should be cut, thus forming a T. It must be the same depth as the first slot and should rise to the surface at as shallow an angle as possible. Doing this

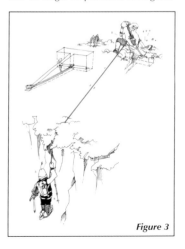

Figure 3

60

is not easy, and is furthered hindered by the coils around the rescuer's shoulders. These can be slipped over the head to leave the upper body free.

When the slot is prepared, a Larks Foot or Clove Hitch is put around the axe at approximately two-thirds of the way up the shaft towards the head (this is to provide an equal bearing surface to prevent the axe from pivoting). The axe is pushed horizontally into the head of the slot and the sling laid into the right-angle slot. A krab is clipped to the sling. A prussik loop is tied in an autobloc/French prussik around the tight rope as close as possible to the krab and then clipped to this. Now the prussik is pushed forward as tight as possible, and the rescuer should slide forward gently to transfer the victim's weight to the autobloc. The shoulder coils can be undone and removed methodically, and finally the rope on the slack side of the autobloc should be clipped through the krab. This is now referred to as a clutch.

Preparation for hoisting: For the rescuer to operate in safety he must be attached to the belay (see Figure 4). The easiest way to do this is to untie from the end of the rope and clip this to the belay. He should then attach himself to the rope via an Italian Hitch into the screwgate krab on his harness. He must carefully approach the edge of the crevasse, paying out the rope through the hitch (effectively

Figure 4

abseiling though not necessarily weighting the belay). Having ascertained that the victim needs pulling out, the edge of the crevasse must be prepared by pushing trekking poles under the rope as near to the edge as possible to prevent further cutting into the lip. The remaining snow lip can be broken away. The frightened victim must now be told to remove his snow-shoes and to clip these, along with his ice-axe and pole, to his harness.

The 3:1 hoist: If the rope hasn't bitten too far into the lip, or if the weight/strength difference of the walkers isn't to the rescuer's disadvantage, it should be possible to lift the victim using a 3:1 pulley system (sometimes referred to as a Z pulley) (see Figure 5a). A second prussik loop is tied onto the taut rope close to the

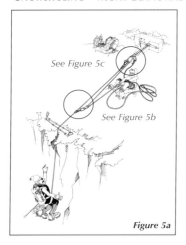

See Figure 5c

See Figure 5b

Figure 5a

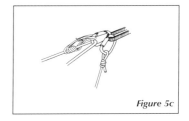

Figure 5c

pulley has been pulled up tight against the belay, the clutch can be used to hold the victim whilst the pulley is slid back down the rope to start again.

The 6:1 hoist: If the 3:1 hoist doesn't work it can be quickly turned into a 6:1 (see Figure 6). The third prussik loop is tied onto the rope as it exits the pulley, and the third krab is clipped to it. The other end of the rope, which up to now has protected

poles at the lip, and a krab and pulley clipped to it. The slack rope from the clutch can now be clipped through the pulley. Pulling the rope back towards the belay now gives a mechanical advantage of 3:1. As the victim moves upwards the autobloc forming the clutch slackens and allows the rope to run through it. When the rescuer tires he can gently release the load and the clutch will reactivate and hold the victim's weight again. Similarly, when the

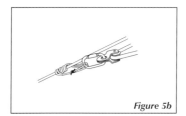

Figure 5b

Figure 6

the rescuer, can be clipped through the third krab. Pulling on this results in a 6:1 system. The rescuer will have a fair amount of running around to do, as for every 6m of rope he pulls in the victim will rise only 1m.

Finally, as the victim nears the lip the rescuer will have to try to extract the rope from where it has bitten in by pulling and bracing his feet against the wall of the crevasse. At the last moment the rescuer may be able to crawl forward to help the victim out.

It's vital to be experienced in glacier travel before venturing out there (photo: Francine Pasche)

GLACIER TRAVEL CHECKLIST

Crampons

Ice axe – 55–60cm for a normal-sized person

Harness
Crevasse rescue equipment:
- 2 prussik loops
- long sling
- 5 karabiners (1 screwgate, 1 pear-shaped screwgate (HMS) which can be used for an Italian hitch, 3 snaplinks)
- ice screw.

This is a minimum of rescue equipment, and you may choose to take other things.

Rope – this should be a dynamic rope of at least 8mm, and a minimum of about 30m long.

Clearly if there are lots of people in the group more than one rope should be taken, but bear in mind that weight is also an issue. Note that the down side of a thin rope is that it is harder to grip for rescue manoeuvres, both by hand and with prussiks.

Finally, be sure to practise all glacier travel techniques before venturing onto glacier terrain.

SNOWSHOE DESIGN

Over the centuries snowshoes have changed and developed enormously. From the first wood-frame shoes, with a deck of bark, rawhide or vines, this rudimentary equipment has now evolved into a whole range of technical snowshoes.

There are different snowshoes for the various types of snowshoeing: **beginners**, who will be snowshoeing on the flat, possibly even on trails specially made for this activity; **recreational snowshoers**, who don't plan to look for difficult slopes or demanding terrain; **alpine snowshoers**, who intend to go high, perhaps to do summits and glacier travel or to use their snowshoes for approaches to ice climbs or snowboard descents, or for treks where they will certainly encounter many types of terrain; and **snowshoe runners**.

Before buying snowshoes you must decide which category you fall into, or buy a general snowshoe that is good for most terrain. One of the biggest problems is sorting through the incredible selection of snowshoes on the market. This is the result of the tremendous growth in this industry, and from the tailoring of designs to specific needs. You can't really choose a pair of snowshoes without understanding the basic design and the variations on that.

American and Canadian snowshoes tend to differ somewhat from European ones, although now most major US companies sell their snowshoes in Europe and vice versa.

It is still possible to find traditional wooden snowshoes, at least in the USA, although even these are very different from the early models. However, so many other types are available that it's worth considering all the options before deciding that one style is best. One major reason for the development of snowshoes is the change from survival use to sporting use. Previously the use of snowshoes was very limited, the oval wooden variety being only really effective on flat plateau terrain, above the treeline, where floatation is the only consideration. Since the development of snowshoeing as a sport, hikers are venturing into more and more varied terrain which makes different demands on snowshoes.

Shape: Early on, the North American hunters saw the limitations of the round snowshoes and experimented with an oval shape, made of two branches, with a long tail which helped to give the snowshoe more stability. These were fine for terrain that was flat with no obstacles. To cope with steeper ground, traverses and forests, snowshoes have become smaller, waisted, with a turned-up toe, and sometimes asymmetrical. The asymmetrical shoes have different shapes for the right and left foot, promoting a natural stride, and are designed to allow the user to keep his feet closer together, but there can be some loss of flotation as the shoes are smaller in the middle.

64

All this makes for a shoe that can climb up and down efficiently, and can cross slopes and negotiate fallen trees and bushes. However, it should be remembered that there is some ground that snowshoes just can't cope with, and this is where you take them off or turn back.

The material: Wood is perfect for large snowshoes, but for technical ground a lighter shoe is preferable. In America this has taken the form of an aluminium tube frame, with a deck made of synthetic material, laced to the frame. In Europe plastic frames were introduced in the 1970s and are now also quite common in the USA, although the aluminium frame is equally popular there. In my experience the aluminium frame is good in deep snow but doesn't provide as

much traction on steeper hard snow. However, brands do vary, and each person must make his own decision.

The deck: The deck is the centre panel of material attached to the frame, providing the snowshoe's flotation. With a plastic shoe this is formed by injection moulding, and so appears to be part of the frame. With aluminium or wooden frames the deck is attached to the frame by some sort of lacing. Most manufacturers have a heel strike plate on the deck of their snowshoes, which keeps the heel of the boot from sliding on the deck surface. Without this the foot will be unstable on anything but flat ground.

The pivot system and binding: Snowshoes are designed so that the foot can roll from heel to toe with

Choose a binding that fits your boot

65

each step, just like a normal walking gait. To allow this to happen there is a hole in the deck which the toe goes through with each step. The foot is held on the shoe by some form of binding, and the way in which this is attached to the snowshoe is fundamental to the performance of the shoe.

The attachment point where the toe rolls through the shoe is known as the pivot point. A **rotating-pivot system** consists of a metal rod onto which the binding is attached. This allows the planted foot to rotate down through the toe-hole as the other foot is moving forward.

The deck of the snowshoe has free movement, and when the snowshoe is lifted forward the tail of the snowshoe drops downwards, rotating around the pivot rod, as the tail naturally remains in the snow. This means that excess snow sheds off the deck easily and that the shoe doesn't have to be lifted to move forward. It also makes for very efficient climbing of steep slopes when the toe is used to make small steps straight up the slope. However, the downside is that the shoe is less manoeuvrable in tight places or among bushes and trees. Some rotating-pivot systems are a variation of this and allow limited movement of the deck, which can make for better handling.

A **fixed-pivot system** is generally easier to manoeuvre than the rotating system. The fixed pivot is a flexible strap onto which the binding is mounted. This system also allows the toe of the planted foot to rotate down through the toe-hole as the other foot moves forward. However, the fixed pivot greatly restricts the mobility of the deck, which does not freely rotate downwards. Instead, to make the forward stride the whole of the snowshoe must be lifted. Clearly this can be difficult in deep snow, but it can make life easier when trying to reverse out of a cul-de-sac or when clambering over obstacles.

Some designs now offer a dual system, incorporating the best of both these systems. There are also spring bindings and bindings that can be clipped down to the deck in situations where you don't want any downward movement.

If you know that you will only snowshoe on prepared trails, then your choice is easy and you'll choose the fixed pivot. If you expect to do the majority of your snowshoe hiking above the tree-line in deep snow, then you'll choose the rotating pivot. However most people have to make a compromise on this, choosing the shoe that best fits most of their requirements.

The binding: There are many different ways of attaching the foot to the snowshoe. The most important criteria is that feet stay attached to the shoe in all conditions. A good binding must provide a reliable connection between the boot and the snowshoe, not allowing any snow build up between the two, and must not

66

require constant adjustment. The binding must also provide lateral stability, so that your feet stay stable on steep slopes, up and down, and on traverses. Some bindings have toe and heel straps, some also an instep strap. Others feature a toe glove; others are step-in like a crampon. There are some that are made for snowboarding boots and some for which you have to buy special boots. Be sure before buying that the binding is compatible with your boots and with the type of snowshoeing that you plan to do. If you normally walk with your feet pointing out or in, some bindings might suit you better than others – on snowshoes you have no choice but to walk with your feet facing forwards, but some bindings cope better with this problem than others. Beginner bindings, and those available on some rental snowshoes, are often very basic and are inadequate on anything except totally flat trails.

Traction devices: All except beginner snowshoes now feature some form of traction device, usually under the toe-hole and often also either along the sides of the shoe and/or at the heel.

These devices range from crampons to studs to cleats, and some are much more solid than others.

The **forward traction device** under the ball of the foot is the main one, and it should be big enough to provide effective grip on the type of slope that you're likely to walk on. If you plan on staying on relatively level terrain then this doesn't need to be very chunky, but if you're aiming to do summits you need a front traction device that will bite, even into hard snow.

Lateral traction devices are for traversing, to prevent the snowshoe from slipping sideways, and since snowshoes do not excel at lateral traction this will never be perfect. The heel traction device helps with traversing and also provides better control during descents.

Some aluminium or wood snowshoes benefit from the traction provided by the lacing of the deck to the frame, and some decks even have a special textured underside that increases traction.

Heel-lift: The heel-lift is a step that can be put up under the heel of the binding which effectively raises the

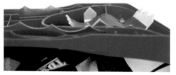

Traction devices are essential if you are to do any snowshoeing on slopes

snowshoer's heel when walking uphill, thus reducing muscle fatigue. Snowshoes with a soft deck do not have this feature, which can be a drawback in certain conditions. Try a pair with and without before buying.

There are many other specialisations: some snowshoes allow for the wearing of crampons, others are specially adapted for use in other sports such as snowboarding; some fold up, some have padded bindings; there are snowshoes for running and snowshoes for children; snowshoes that come with extensions, and snowshoes that turn into a shovel, not to mention all manner of colours and shapes.

When you've decided what features are important for the snowshoeing that you plan to do there are several other considerations.

Weight of the snowshoes: It is said that 1 kilo on your feet is worth 5 kilos on your back, and with this in mind, whatever your projected snowshoeing activities, it is worth considering the weight of the snowshoes that you use, and the boots you'll use with them. Whilst you can't compromise on boots, you can choose the lightest snowshoes that meet your requirements. This is especially relevant for smaller people. Larger people should beware, though, not to sacrifice flotation for lighter weight.

Weight of the snowshoer: Be sure to get snowshoes that are the right size

for your weight – and be aware that if you have the good fortune to usually experience lots of cold bottomless powder, you could probably use snowshoes with more flotation than someone who often snowshoes hard technical slopes.

Most snowshoes come in at least two sizes, the first being adequate in normal conditions for an adult person up to around 175lbs/80kg. The next size up is for larger people, or could be used in deep snow conditions or when the snow is very warm and wet. Some snowshoes come with removable extensions for such conditions. Children's snowshoes exist, but for children over about 100lbs/45kg the smaller adult size is fine.

It should be understood that in certain conditions you are going to sink into the snow whatever you've got on your feet. In this case find someone else to make the track!

Cost: In general, plastic-frame snowshoes tend to be at the lower end of the price range, although even these increase dramatically in price for the more specialised versions. Aluminium frames are slightly more expensive, with traditional wood-frame snowshoes topping the price range.

Some large outdoor retailers make their own brands of snowshoes, and these are fine if you're looking for a beginner's or recreational snowshoe, or snowshoes for children. However, for alpine snowshoeing it is important to be sure that the snowshoes are reliable, durable and have specialised bindings and traction devices. These will almost always be better on snowshoes made by reputable snowshoe manufacturers who have long-term experience in this field. You should also check out guarantee and replacement of parts.

Fit: It is important that your snowshoes fit your boots. Check that the toe of your boot can go all the way into the toe binding, so that the ball of your foot is positioned over the pivot rod/strap, still allowing your toe to rotate through the toe-hole when you step forward. This can be a problem with large padded boots, such as snowboarding boots, or for people with large feet.

SNOWSHOE TECHNIQUE

Although it is true that walking on snowshoes is an extension of walking, and that only a few steps separate the beginner from the established snowshoer, certain techniques are necessary to enable efficient travel on slopes up, down and across, and in tight places. You may choose to discover these techniques either by trial and error or by reading the following tips (thus avoiding too any embarrassing – or worse – incidents). However you decide to progress, always assess the terrain awaiting you and decide how to make the best use of your snowshoes, even if this means removing them. Be sure to stay off technical terrain until you have the necessary

Very nice if you can do it!

experience and the right conditions. Don't blindly follow other snow-shoers' tracks – just because they have traversed a slope doesn't mean it will be safe for you – they may have been terrified but still left a perfect line of snowshoe prints!

Putting on your snowshoes: This might seem obvious, but it's advisable to figure out how to put on your snowshoes before setting out in the snow. It's easier to read the instructions and to adjust straps in the comfort of your warm living room than all trussed up in mittens, balaclava and duvet jacket in deep powder snow. If there is a right and left shoe (as in asymmetrical frames) be aware of this. Symmetrical frames are identical, but there will be a right and left where there are buckles to fasten – these should normally close on the outside.

You need to make sure that you push your toe into the binding so that the ball of your foot is over the pivot rod or pivot strap, but that your toe

can still rotate through the toe-hole when you walk.

Walking: If you're on a made trail you won't find a lot of difference between walking on snowshoes and walking on dry ground. Most properly sized snowshoes allow for a natural stride, especially those with aluminium or plastic frames. However, as soon as you are on untracked snow you will always find that you sink in to some degree – snowshoes don't prevent sinking they minimise it. The extent to which you sink will be affected by the size of your snowshoe in relation to your weight, the type of snow (wet or dry), and the type of snowshoes.

Breaking trail can be strenuous, depending on the depth and wetness of the snow, and on the type of snow-shoe you have. Always go steadily and make an effort to put one foot in front of the other, making a neat, narrow track. Look ahead for the direction you want to take and head for it in the easiest line, rather then weav-

Descending, traversing (note pole gripped low down) and manoeuvring (pp.70 and 71)

ing around and wasting energy. Don't lift your snowshoes higher than you need to – if you have rotating pivots, try to master the technique of letting the snowshoe drag in the snow as you make a stride forward.

In wet snow or conditions where the temperature changes fast, you may find lumps of wet snow building up on the deck of the shoe or on the traction devices underneath. You need to stop to clear this periodically – if it builds up under the foot plate of a binding or on the sole of your boot you could put enormous leverage on the toe binding and some types could be damaged by this. Be careful to avoid putting your snowshoes into streams, as the water will quickly form ice, which is very difficult to remove.

When manoeuvring in tight spaces the type of pivot system you have will make a lot of difference. If you have the facility to clip down the binding to the deck this can make it much easier to pick up the shoe to step over obstacles or to reverse. This can be crucial if searching for an avalanche victim, for example.

Instead of reversing out of a tight place, you might perfect the 'kick turn' (see Figure 7): lift up one snowshoe so that it is vertical; then turn it 180° and plant it firmly in the snow. Next swing the other snowshoe around and place it beside the reversed one. You can do this facing into or out from the slope, but the former is more usual on steep slopes. Practice kick turns first on easy ground!

Figure 7 – Kick turn

Ascending steep slopes: How you climb depends on snow conditions, the angle of the slope, your snowshoes and your preference. Gentle slopes can be climbed directly or by zigzagging. If you have heel-lifts on your snowshoes, you'll probably be happy to use them. Steeper slopes, especially those that are hard-packed, require a more aggressive approach. It will probably be necessary to climb such slopes face-on using the toes of your boots. The best snowshoe design for this is the rotating pivot: your toe goes through the toe-hole of the shoe unrestricted by the deck, which hangs parallel to the slope, allowing optimum grip by the front traction device. With fixed-pivot devices you just need to be sure that your front traction device is gripping properly before you take your next step up.

In some snow it is possible to kick a step using your snowshoe, especially with a fixed-pivot design, where the toe of the snowshoe can be used to make a platform to step up. But this is usually very energy-consuming.

Descending steep slopes: Traction devices, both forward and rear, along with a confident approach, help to maintain control on descents. Keeping your weight over your knees, it is often possible to make a platform for each step down by digging in the heels of your snowshoes. The traction devices should grip easily if the snow is at all hard – in icy conditions you should probably be wearing crampons not snowshoes.

Deep powder snow sometimes allows you to run down the slope with great loping strides – not only is this fun but it's also much faster. Again a confident approach pays off, but before lurching down any slope be sure that it's not likely to avalanche.

Crusty or heavy snow is relatively easy to descend if you plunge your feet into the snow.

Always keep the tips of the snowshoes up, otherwise you'll take a nose dive.

Traversing steep slopes: Traversing is the one major weakness of snowshoes and can be very dangerous. Traversing

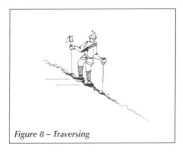

Figure 8 – Traversing

should be avoided if the slope is icy and the consequences of a fall not good.

You traverse a slope one of two ways. The first option is to create a platform for your snowshoes – this is done by kicking the side of the snowshoes into the slope (see Figure 8). Some shoes are better for this than others, especially those with lateral traction devices. Aluminium frames are notoriously insecure on traverses in anything but deep snow. If you make a platform for both feet at the same level traversing can be quite comfortable, but if one foot is higher than the other this is very tiring on the higher leg. In this case you may try to walk across putting one leg directly in front of the other. However, this does require a certain amount of balance and you can trip up over your shoes.

The second option is to put the whole base of your shoe on the slope and hope it grips (see Figure 9). Some shoes are designed for this with excellent lateral traction devices, but the angle of slope and type of snow are crucial to success.

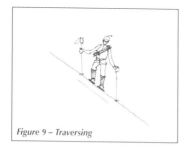

Figure 9 – Traversing

If in doubt go straight up a slope rather than traverse it, or take off snowshoes and use crampons in icy conditions. If it is not possible to cross a slope safely you must look for an alternative.

Even armed with these techniques, be very cautious on steep slopes. Even the best snowshoes can't compensate for a lack of experience or save you from an avalanche. Make sure you have sufficient expertise before attempting a steep slope, and be aware of avalanche risks. Some slopes are just not made for snowshoes, and should only be tackled using crampons and ice-axe or not at all.

Getting back up: Snowshoeing is not an activity where you would expect to fall a lot, but you certainly will end up in the snow at some point, usually as a result of having fun, such as running down a slope. The falling bit is easy and almost always totally pain-free, but the getting back up can be quite a performance, especially in deep snow. If there's

Falling down is the easy part

73

The mountains at their best – here near the Tête de Balme (Route 28)

someone around to give a hand then that's fine. If not, you need to use your poles, either by planting them in the snow to support you or by laying them on the snow's surface in an X pattern to get additional flotation – press down on these as you lever yourself up. In extreme circumstances you may have to remove your pack if it's heavy.

Final word: After all this technique remember that snowshoeing is a natural and beautiful form of travel in the snow. Keep your track in tune with the surroundings, following the gentle contours of the terrain, and take pride in making your track elegant and unobtrusive. If there's already a track, why make another one? When descending be sure to leave some untracked snow for the enjoyment of the next snowshoers or skiers.

WINTER CODE OF GOOD CONDUCT
How to have fun winter walking, remaining safe and respectful of nature

The code of conduct below is taken from that issued by the French Accompagnateurs en Montagne.

Be conscious of the dangers: Fog, hard icy slopes, stream beds, lakes, avalanches, the cold, summer paths unpassable in winter, wind, intense sun, hidden rocks and fences … there are many dangers to be aware of.

Be well equipped: Use clothes and equipment that are adapted for winter conditions. Be sure to take enough food and drink. Be sure to have appropriate safety equipment – map, first aid, survival bag, rope, avalanche transceiver, shovel and probe, depending on the nature of the walk.

Be respectful and aware of nature: Find out about any areas that have restricted access. Try to avoid disturbing the animals, which are already in a fragile state in the winter. Don't leave the route just to get a close-up view of a creature – binoculars are sufficient. Respect the tranquillity of the mountains and take care with young trees and vegetation.

Be respectful of others: The ski pistes are primarily for skiers, and the cross-country trails are easily broken down by snowshoers and walkers. Many people go to the mountains for peace and silence.

Be aware of your tracks: One track in virgin snow is beautiful, ten different ones not so good.

Be well informed: Take note of the conditions and the weather forecast. Speak to the experts – mountain leaders and guides, ski patrollers, park wardens, etc.

Sur le Rocher and the Aiguille Verte behind (Route 25)

FRANCE
Cluses/Sallanches Region

Cluses
When you reach Cluses you really feel as though the mountains are distant. They are actually not far away, but most people would probably prefer to base themselves at higher altitude away from the humdrum reminders of normal life.

Beaufort
Quite a drive south from Cluses, Beaufort is the centre for the Beaufortain area. The town is of a reasonable size and offers all services. There are numerous other possibilities around Beaufort itself.

Morzine
The classic bustling ski resort, Morzine nevertheless offers a good base for snowshoeing, being close to Les Gets, Samoëns and other walking areas. Plenty of hotels and apartments and all necessary facilities.

Samoëns
Samoëns is a pleasant town, old and interesting with small winding streets and a sense of tradition. It is well situated for walks to the north and east of Cluses. Also close by is Sixt-Fer-à-Cheval, with its imposing cirque.

Sallanches
Sallanches itself is the first big town you come to when descending the Arve valley from Chamonix. Whilst it is well positioned for shops and restaurants, it is a little industrialised for a base.

Les Contamines-Montjoie
This is a pleasant small town with plenty of amenities. Although there is a ski area nearby this does not dominate the town, and there are a variety of walks to be done from here.

St Gervais-les-Bains
Famous for its thermal baths, St Gervais is an interesting old town, very popular in winter with British skiers. This means that there are lots of activities, day and night.

Megève
Megève is known for its plush restaurants and hotels, famously patronised by the Rothschilds and Sasha Distel, among others. However, it caters for everyone, and there is no shortage of eateries and bars. It is quite large and enjoys an active winter clientele.

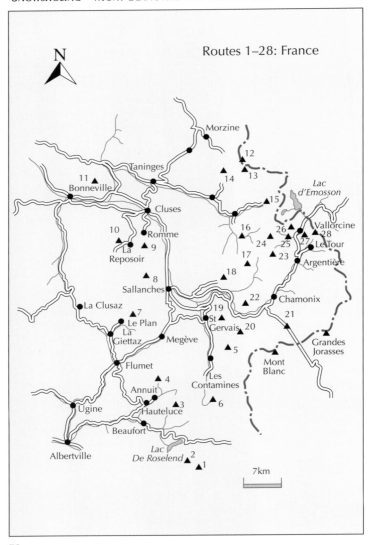

Routes 1–28: France

1: Combe de la Neuva and Col du Grand Fond, 2671m

Starting point	Cormet de Roseland
Starting altitude	1967m
Summit altitude	2671m
Altitude gain	704m
Time	5h round trip
Grade	2
Aspect	NE
Map	1:25,000 IGN Top 25 3532 OT Beaufortain
Accommodation	Refuge de Presset – open but not wardened in winter

Access: From Beaufort drive up over the Col de Méraillet to the car park at Cormet de Roseland. For road conditions tel Beaufort Tourist Office: 0479383757

The Combe de la Neuva is a superb long valley, impressive and rocky, enclosed by steep slopes on both sides. This gives a magnificent walk, penetrating right into the heart of the mountains. Such valleys do present a great risk of avalanche in unstable conditions, so save this walk for days when the snow is not going to shift. If you go as far as the Col du Grand Fond you will have good views of the famous Pierra Menta. This unusual conglomerate monolith is surprisingly well known. Standing as it does above the tranquil pasture land of the Beaufortain, the Pierra Menta provides a rugged contrast to the rolling hills below. Legend has it that Gargantua, whilst crossing the Alps towards what is now Italy, was stopped in his tracks by the snowy mass of the Mont Blanc massif. He searched for a way through to the right and tripped over the Aravis range. In anger he kicked the mountains, and sent a piece of rock flying through the air to land in the heart of the Beaufortain, leaving a *brêche* on the Aravis ridge, which is now known as the Porte des Aravis, and creating the Pierra Menta.

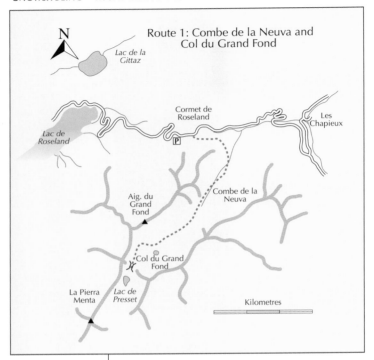

As with all walks in this area, it can only be undertaken in the spring when the road has been cleared of snow. You must check that the Col de Méraillet is open – this usually happens in early spring. If it is not possible to drive up to Cormet de Roseland it may be necessary to park at the Col des Sauces and continue on foot. Beware of avalanches from the slopes of the Roc du Biolley.

Route
From the Cormet de Roseland, take the track which goes around the hillside under the slopes of the Dent d'Arpire and into the Combe de la Neuva. There are steep slopes above, so do not go here after fresh snowfall.

The way is easy to see, as it basically follows the valley. At the head of the valley enter a cirque, defined by the Aiguille du Grand Fond, the Pointe de Presset, the Aiguille de la Nova and the Col de la Nova.

Alpine Chough getting airtime

To reach the vantage point of the Col du Grand Fond, 2671m, climb up the slopes on your right, under the Brèche de Parozan, to about 2550m, then traverse under the Pointe Presset and up to the Col. Directly ahead to the south is the Pierra Menta and, beyond, the Isére valley and the Vanoise National Park. Just below can be seen the Refuge de Presset, but if you want to go down to this, better to take the neighbouring Col de Petit Fond, 2622m (not named on the map), which provides an easier way through.

Return by the same valley, varying the way a little as you wish.

2: Grande Berge du Lac de Roseland, 2089m

Starting point	Les Sauces
Starting altitude	1645m
Summit altitude	2089m
Altitude gain	460m
Time	4h–4h30
Grade	1
Aspect	N, W
Map	1:25,000 IGN Top 25 3532 OT Beaufortain

Access: Park at Les Sauces, 1645m. For road conditions tel. Beaufort Tourist Office: 0479383757

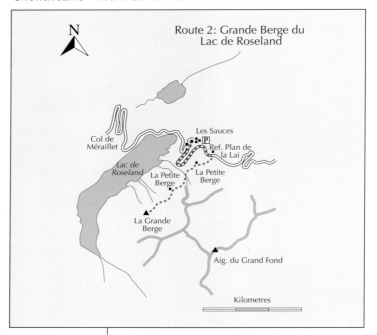

Route 2: Grande Berge du Lac de Roseland

N

Col de
Méraillet

Les Sauces

P

Ref. Plan de
la Lai

Lac de
Roseland

La Petite
Berge

La Petite
Berge

La Grande
Berge

Aig. du Grand Fond

Kilometres

The south-east bank of the Roseland lake provides beautiful walking terrain, especially in winter, and the rounded summit of Grande Berge, 2089m, is a good objective for a pleasant day's snowshoeing, with superb views of the lake to the east, and the surrounding mountains to the north and south.

Access to this area is difficult in winter and you should check that the Col de Méraillet has been cleared of snow – this usually happens in early spring.

Route

Follow the road up past the Roc de Biolley to reach the Refuge Plan de la Lai, 1818m. Here leave the road to head south-west, already enjoying extensive views, to the chalets of La Petite Berge. A short climb takes you to the Petite Berge summit at 2071m. A gentle, undulating traverse continues in the same direction to attain the Grande Berge summit, 2089m, with a chalet close by. It is possible to continue on beyond this, even as far as L'Entrus on the far side of the lake if you wish. Return by the same route.

3: Lac de la Girotte, 1753m, and Col du Sallestet, 2111m

Starting point	Les Granges
Starting altitude	1150m
Summit altitude	2111m
Altitude gain	961m
Time	5h round trip
Grade	1
Aspect	N, W
Map	1:25,000 IGN Top 25 3531 OT Megève Col des Aravis; 1:50,000 Didier Richard C Mont Blanc

Access: From Beaufort drive up to Hauteluce and onwards to Saint Sauveur. Continue on this road to the hamlet of Les Granges. Park here.

This is an area of rolling hills and inviting cols, with wide distant views stretching as far as the Mont Blanc massif and beyond. Indeed from here the views of Mont Blanc are some of the best you'll get, and the angle is such that the summit is almost unrecognisably steep and spectacular. With its forests, alpages, gentle slopes and huge, frozen lake this is typical of all that the Beaufortain region has to offer. A paradise for snowshoers.

Route
Leave Les Granges heading south-east following the footpath as well as possible just next to the trees. Come to a narrow and deep hole, which is avoided, and find a way up through the woods on the left. Keep following the path, which remains on the edge of the forest, heading east and passing the small buildings of La Montaz.

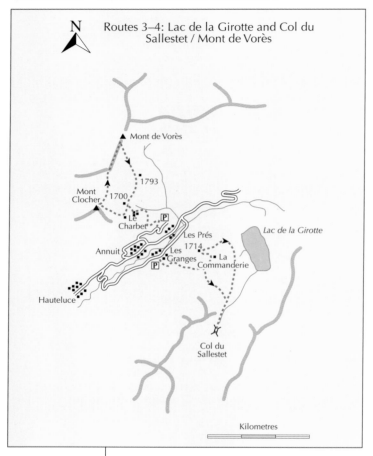

N

Routes 3–4: Lac de la Girotte and Col du Sallestet / Mont de Vorès

Mont de Vorès

1793

Mont Clocher

1700

Le Charbet

P

Les Prés

1714

Annuit

Les Granges

La Commanderie

P

Lac de la Girotte

Hauteluce

Col du Sallestet

Kilometres

Continue on the path as best you can. It swings round to north-east and crosses a short section of woods to finally reach a clearing and the chalets of La Commanderie. Head west past an isolated chalet at pt 1714, then follow the partly wooded rounded shoulder eastwards to contour round the north side of the obvious hill marked pt

1926 and find the frozen Lac de la Girotte beneath you. Continue to circumnavigate the hill and go over the small col at 1869m. From here head south towards the Plan de la Mouille and on up to the Col du Sallestet. Spread out ahead to the south are all the peaks of the Beaufortain, and in the distance is the Vanoise range.

Return to the Plan de la Mouille and descend north-west down into the Combe de l'Alpettaz to reach a large forest track at pt 1701. Follow this rightwards until you rejoin the ascent itinerary just below La Commanderie. Return to Les Granges.

4: Mont de Vorès, 2067m

Starting point	Pylon on road above Les Prés
Starting altitude	1310m
Summit altitude	2067m
Altitude gain	816m
Time	6h round trip
Grade	2
Aspect	S, SW
Map	1:25,000 IGN Top 25 3531 OT Megève; 1:50,000 Didier Richard C Mont Blanc

Access: From Beaufort drive up to Hauteluce then on towards Annuit. Before this village is reached take a small road on the left, which climbs up above the village. Turn right at a junction onto a road above the hamlet of Les Prés. Park not far from an electricity pylon at 1310m.

For the best views of the Mont Blanc massif you need to be somewhat distant from it, and this walk proves the case. Mont de Vorès (also known as Tête des 3 Coins) offers a most fantastic panoramic vista. It takes in not just the Mont Blanc massif but also, across the Arly valley, the Aravis range dominated by the Pointe Percée, further north the huge Rochers des Fiz, and to the south the Beaufortain peaks such as the Aiguille du Grand Fond and, very clearly, the Col du Bonhomme.

The walk takes place almost entirely on open slopes, which means that you have plenty of time to savour this visual treat opening up before you as you climb. From

Running is often the easiest – and definitely the most fun – way to descend

the first summit of Mont Clocher rounded ridges lead to Mont de Vorès, and only increase the impression of airiness – your eyes and camera will be on overload here, so don't go on a cloudy day!

It is perhaps a shame that the ski lifts of Notre Dame de Bellecombe have spread to include the north slopes of Mont de Vorès, but they don't detract from the views, as the walk is described from the other side. If you can go early in the winter the lifts won't even be open.

Bear in mind that the majority of this walk faces south and consequently get lots of sun. Later in the season there may not be much snow left.

Route

From the pylon set off north-east on a track which doubles back to more or less follow the electricity cables. This leads past some chalets and then onwards to the chalets of Le Charbet. Continue in the same line above the chalets, making a right turn into the forest to then emerge at more chalets at 1700m. Go south to the isolated chalet of Lousteta, then follow the shoulder west to the summit of Mont Clocher, 1976m.

A large rounded ridge leads north at first in a gentle descent. Do not take the track (not always visible in the snow), but continue north to the small highpoint 2061, where the lift arrives from the other side. Be sure to check out the characteristic rocky bastion of the Pierra Menta seen to the south from here, as it is not so obvious from the summit. The way onwards is obvious along the crest to the east, slightly down then up again to the summit of Mont de Vorès.

To descend retrace your steps along the ridge a little before descending directly to the left (south) by easy and pleasant slopes as far as the isolated chalet at pt 1793. Continue down to the tree-line then head along a track which takes you just above the forest, past a slightly more difficult section of slope, all the way back to the chalet at pt 1700 that you passed on the way up. Follow the ascent route for the rest of the way.

5: Mont Truc, 1811m

Access: From Les Contamines-Montjoie drive north and take the road up to La Gruvaz. Park at the end of the road next to the river.

Starting point	La Gruvaz (it is also possible to start directly from Les Contamines-Montjoie, going up past La Frasse)
Starting altitude	1100m
Summit altitude	1811m
Altitude gain	711m
Time	4h round trip
Grade	1
Aspect	W
Map	1:25,000 IGN Top 25 3531 ET St-Gervais-les-Bains; 1:50,000 Didier Richard C Mont Blanc

In standard French the word *truc* means 'thing', and for a long time I thought this summit was Mount Thingy. However, I discovered after further research that in this context *truc* is a patois word for 'dome', and Mont Truc is certainly well named. This relatively modest summit lies just off the famous summer Tour du Mont Blanc trek to the west of the huge glaciated Dômes de Miage, themselves outliers of the Mont Blanc massif.

Whilst Mont Truc is certainly not the most demanding peak, it is a good objective for days when the risk of avalanche is quite high or when the snow level is reasonably low, or just consider it as an accessible walk which gives unforgettable views.

I've been here in all conditions, often bad ones (as the terrain is not too steep), and have been rewarded with sightings of chamois and ibex as well as the immensely impressive glaciers of the west faces of the Dômes de Miage and the adjoining Aiguille de Bionnassay.

This is a walk to savour slowly, beginning in the valley, following an ancient track up past isolated chalets, a reminder of times gone by when people scraped out a

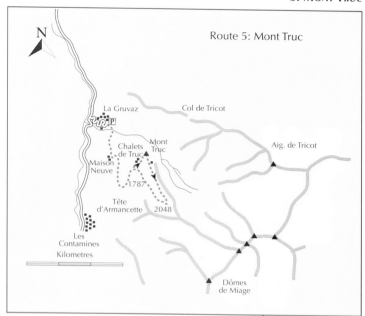

Route 5: Mont Truc

harsh existence from the earth. Higher, the path takes an
easy line through the forest, giving occasional glimpses
of the valley below until the trees start to thin and you
reach the attractive farm buildings of Le Truc, an obvious
picnic stop. The summit is just behind the chalets and is
quickly reached. From the top it is possible to continue
south-east to the spot height 2048 to further enjoy this
spectacular situation.

Route

Cross the river and take the large track that goes into the
forest. You'll soon reach the cluster of chalets at Maison
Neuve, at least one of which has been permanently
inhabited recently. Go up behind the chalets, still on a
good track. This continues to a junction where the
Chalets de Truc are signposted to the right. Continue to

On the summit of
Mont Truc

another junction, this time going left. (This is where the path up from Les Contamines-Montjoie comes in.) The trail climbs at a steady grade to reach the Chalets de Truc. The route to Mont Truc is obvious. Having climbed this come back down heading south-east to an isolated chalet then continue on to go up to pt 2048.

From here a direct descent north-west will take you to a large boulder marked pt 1787 on the map, right on the edge of the forest. From here it is simple to rejoin the track on which you came up. Return by the same route.

6: Lacs Jovet, 2174m, and Monts Jovet, 2362m

The Monts Jovet are twin summits forming a long ridge tucked away at the head of the Contamines valley. To go all the way to the summits of Monts Jovet is a very long undertaking, but there is the choice of stopping at Lacs Jovet, or Plan Jovet, just above the Chalets de

Starting point	Notre Dame de la Gorge
Starting altitude	1210m
Summit altitude	Lacs Jovet 2174m, Monts Jovet south summit 2362m
Altitude gain	760m for Lacs Jovet, 1152m for Monts Jovet
Time	5h30 Plan Jovet, 8h Monts Jovet.
Grade	Plan Jovet 2, Monts Jovet 3
Aspect	N, W, S
Map	1:25,000 IGN Top 25 3531 ET St-Gervais-les-Bains and 3531 OT Megève; 1:50,000 Didier Richard C Mont Blanc
Public transport	Bus Les Contamines–Les Pontets, about 1km from Notre Dame de la Gorge

Access: From Les Contamines continue south out of town to the large parking at Notre Dame de la Gorge.

Jovet. Wherever you get to, this whole area is an absolute joy for snowshoers, offering gentle rolling terrain with plenty of possibilities for cutting the walk short, if necessary, and still having an excellent day out. Despite the proximity of the ski area of Les Contamines-Montjoie, just to the west, there's no sign of it here, and the area has a beautifully wild atmosphere.

The approach is by the Roman road, the entry point to the Arve valley for the Romans from what is now the Tarentaise. They soon established their villas on the sunny slopes of nearby Passy. The word Jovet is thought to be an ancient name for Jupiter, who was worshiped by the Romans.

The summit described here is the south summit of the Monts Jovet. This can be traversed on snowshoes by taking the steepish south ridge, then descending via gentler slopes to the Lacs Jovet. This gives a fantastic circuit, and you can even include the subsidiary summit marked pt 2368 on the map.

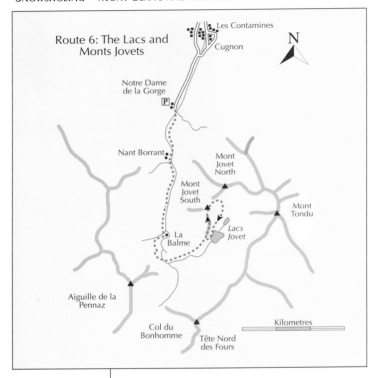

Route 6: The Lacs and Monts Jovets

Les Contamines
Cugnon
N

Notre Dame de la Gorge
P

Nant Borrant

Mont Jovet North

Mont Jovet South

Lacs Jovet

Mont Tondu

La Balme

Aiguille de la Pennaz

Col du Bonhomme

Tête Nord des Fours

Kilometres

Route

Cross over the river by the bridge leading out of the car park then head up the Roman road. This is steep at first but it does ease fairly soon. It can be icy at the bottom, in which case crampons can be useful. (In really icy conditions it may be better to avoid the bottom of the Roman road and to take the steep path on the true left bank of the river via l'Amery and la Chenalettaz.)

After passing the Chalet Nant Borrant on the right, continue along the main track. Where the road flattens at La Rollaz it is possible to divert from the main trail into the trees, and the Chalets at Les Prés make a nice place

Looking south from Monts Jovet to the Col du Bonhomme (photo: Jon de Montjoie)

to stop for a snack if you're just going to the Plan Jovet. From the chalets it is possible to continue above the tree-line under the slopes of the Aiguille de Roselette, returning to the main trail above La Balme. However, those heading for the summit should resist this detour and stay on the main track to make faster time.

Continue heading south above La Balme, under the electricity cables, until you reach the pylon, then head east on flat ground towards the rolling slopes of Plan Jovet. Steeper slopes lead to the snow-covered Lacs Jovet. Before you quite reach these, take a diagonal line up left (west) to attain the south ridge of the south summit. This provides a fine route to the summit in a nicely exposed situation where you can appreciate the views on both sides. It's often breezy here, and on a hot day you will appreciate the chill. From the summit be sure to notice Mont Blanc peeping over the nearer peaks of Mont Tondu and the Pain de Sucre.

Continue north-east into a small col (unnamed on the map, but between the summits of pts 2368 and

Further Options

There are a host of possibilities here – just use your imagination. The north summit of Monts Jovet is a good alternative if there are lots of people heading up to the south summit. The Col du Bonhomme offers extensive views towards the Beaufortain and gives a great descent back down to La Balme.

2428), from where you can easily descend to the lakes. The rest of the descent is more or less by the same route, taking the best slopes according to the snow conditions. If you're lucky there will be soft transformed snow on sunny slopes which will be a delight to descend. Remember there is a lot of mileage in this route, so be sure to leave plenty of daylight for the return.

7: Petit Croisse Baulet, 2009m

Access: From Sallanches drive to Megève then onwards through Praz Arly to Flumet, where you take the road towards the Col des Aravis. At La Giettaz turn right and drive up to the tiny resort of Le Plan. Continue on the small track to La Crepinière. Park here.

Starting point	La Crepinière
Starting altitude	1280m
Summit altitude	2009m
Altitude gain	729m
Time	4h30 round trip
Grade	2
Aspect	W
Map	1:25,000 IGN Top 25 3531 OT Megève; 1:50,000 Didier Richard C Mont Blanc

The Croisse Baulet and Petit Croisse Baulet (sometimes spelt as Croise) stand proud above the Arve valley, and consequently offer exceptional views of the surrounding peaks. The Petit Croisse Baulet, described here, provides the perfect snowshoe walk and, unusually for this altitude, most of the ascent follows a rounded ridge so views can be enjoyed in both directions. This also limits the risk of avalanches, and means this summit can be considered in most conditions.

Starting in the forest, you are quickly above the treeline and can enjoy snowshoeing perfect angle slopes with just the odd bush and tree to add variety. Once on the summit, you will not know which direction to look such is the extent of the panorama here – from Mont Blanc to the Rochers des Fiz to the Aravis range to the depths of the Arve valley.

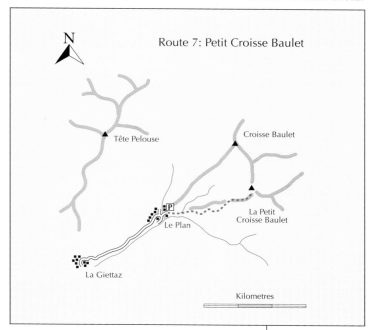

There has been talk of incorporating this area into
the nearby ski resorts and extending the lift systems to
create the Espace Diamant which, it is claimed, will be
the largest ski area in Europe. Let us hope this project
never sees the light of day, since there are already plenty
of ski runs in this region. The Petit Croisse Baulet and its
neighbours are very special summits which deserve to
remain untarnished by lifts and queues.

Route
From La Crepinière there is a footpath signed up through
the woods that is waymarked in blue. Follow this if you
can, although there are numerous possibilities for shortcuts, depending on the snow. You will emerge from the
forest just under the delightful old chalet of La Tourste.

The rounded ridge of the Petit Croisse Baulet makes for a pleasant ascent

Further Options It is perfectly feasible to go on to the Croisse Baulet, which adds another 300m to the ascent. However, this should be avoided in conditions of high avalanche risk, when the final slope can be dangerous.

Already, behind you, there are views of the steep slopes of the Aravis summits.

From the chalet head around rightwards to the rounded ridge leading up to the Tête de Ramadieu. It is best to keep to the shoulder here above a small newer chalet, as the southern slopes of the Tête de Ramadieu are prone to avalanche.

As you approach this small summit your gaze will doubtless be held by the Croisse Baulet, which looks huge from here. The route is delightful, along the gentle crest, weaving in and out of small bushes and trees to reach the Croix de Pierre Faki at 1947m. The summit is just above.

Descent by the same route, or from the cross take the south slopes directly, which provide a great bounding descent as far as the spot height 1815 (named Rocher de la Combette on the 1:25,000 map), which forms a small flat area above the trees. Follow the vague rounded arête south-west and then head westwards to hit the main track in the valley around pt 1415 at the oratory. The track leads back to the car.

8: Mayères, 1563m

Starting point	Burzier
Starting altitude	904m
Summit altitude	1563m
Altitude gain	659m
Time	4h round trip
Grade	1
Aspect	E
Map	1:25,000 IGN Top 25 3430 ET La Clusaz; 1:50,000 Didier Richard C Mont Blanc

Access: From Sallanches drive up in the direction of Doran and park at Burzier.

In the depths of winter, after a huge fall of snow, when the sun comes out and everything is white and beautiful – that's the time to become acquainted with the delights of Mayères. With its incredible panorama of the Mont Blanc massif, this is an extremely popular spot in the summer, when it is accessed not only by walkers but also by four-wheel-drive vehicles and light planes. It is a little quieter in winter, and the ski lifts shown on some maps functioned only for a couple of years and have now been totally dismantled.

You can make this an all-day outing by exploring the slopes nearby, or it can be done in half a day. Whichever you choose be sure to take plenty of film, as the views are spectacular.

Further Options It is also possible to go up to Doran, which is in an interesting position and gives great views of the impressive rocky summit of Pointe Percé. However, it is unwise to venture up to Doran or beyond towards the Col de Doran in anything other than very stable snow conditions, as this road is often avalanched and the Doran valley is flanked on both sides by very steep slopes.

Route
From Burzier take the large forest track up to a junction where Doran is signed to the right and Mayères to the left. Take the track to Mayères and follow it all the way past various chalets. The Tournieux chalet is a restaurant and may be open. They do a snowmobile service for clients, but this seems to be an evening operation and has only a minimal impact on the area at the

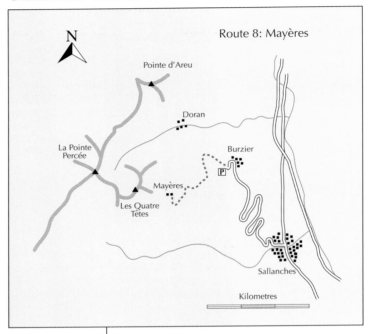

moment. The Chalet Refuge de Mayères is above, and the huge wooden chalet here will be more or less visible depending on the snow cover. It is closed in winter.

Descend by the same route, or head south-east towards La Pechettaz then rejoin the woods, taking a descending traverse left (east) down easy open slopes to reach a small group of chalets at 1329m. At about 1300m, above the isolated chalet of Deramey, which has a cross, traverse around north-east to rejoin the ascent route. Just beyond Les Trépas it is possible to short-cut the track by going down another nice slope to regain the track down to Burzier.

9: *Tête de la Sallaz, 2026m*

Starting point	Romme
Starting altitude	1291m
Summit altitude	2026m
Altitude gain	735m
Time	4h30 round trip
Grade	2
Aspect	N, E
Map	1:25,000 IGN Top 25 3430 ET La Clusaz; 1:50,000 Didier Richard C Mont Blanc

Access: From Cluses take the D4 over the river and under the motorway, then turn sharp left and head uphill on the D119 to Nancy-sur-Cluses. Continue for 4.5km to Romme. Drive through the village, past the ski lift, and at the T-junction turn left towards Le Reposoir. There is a large car park on the right.

The Tête de la Sallaz is situated high above the Arve valley, with its large towns of Cluses and Sallanches sprawling next to the river and hemmed in by the impressive limestone cliffs of this region. The view from the summit is quite simply breathtaking. Having climbed up from the sleepy village of Romme, along forest tracks and clearings, you emerge at a fore-summit marked pt 1919 on the map. Suddenly you are aware of the precipitous drop below and, in the distance, the Mont Blanc massif, seen at its best from here. The Tête de la Sallaz is not far away and a short ascent leads to the rounded summit. Beyond is the impressive rocky Pointe d'Areu, but your gaze will most certainly be held by the glaciated summits glistening in the distance. Mont Blanc presents itself as a high peak, appearing almost pointed from here. To the east the top of the Flaine ski system can be seen and, behind, the Aiguille Verte towers majestically. The Môle, recognisable by its isolated conical summit, seems huge, towering as it does above the valley to the north. Come here in the spring and it will be wearing a snowy cap, whilst all around is snow-free and green.

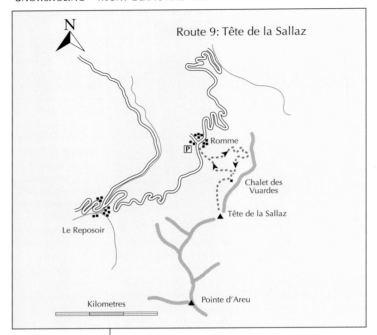

Route 9: Tête de la Sallaz

N

Romme

P

Chalet des Vuardes

Tête de la Sallaz

Le Reposoir

Kilometres

Pointe d'Areu

Route

From the parking area walk along the road a few metres and take the small road on the left. This becomes a track, which is followed across the ski piste. Stay on this track through the forest and you'll arrive eventually at the Chalet des Vuardes. From here the forest thins. Go west, firstly on the forest track then heading up the slopes and out of the trees. The track crosses an obvious rounded ridge and continues rising diagonally, now to the south. The summit of pt 1919 is reached, and ahead lies the Tête de la Sallaz, often sporting a fine cornice on its north face. This should certainly be avoided by gaining the top from the east by the easiest route.

Descend by the same route, perhaps cutting down directly in the forest if the snow is good, as far as the

Chalet des Vuardes. From here you can take the track which comes up to it from the left (looking down). This leads back to the top of the ski piste, which can be descended on the right side (looking down) to the village. Keep well to the edge, and in icy conditions return from the Chalet des Vuardes by the ascent route rather than risking a long slide.

The summit of the Tête de la Sallaz with the Mont Blanc massif behind (photo: Dave Butcher)

10: Petit Bargy, 2098m

Seen from the Arve valley the north face of the Bargy massif, with its Grand and Petit peaks, is very imposing, its impressive rocky slabs sweeping down towards Bonneville. However, the winter access to these summits is from the south side, beginning in the charming village of Le Reposoir, hidden away in the depths of the valley between the Bargy peaks and those of the Aravis.

Positioned as it is, somewhat isolated from the main alpine massifs, the Petit Bargy enjoys magnificent views in all directions, from the castellated skyline of the Aravis

Access: From Cluses take the road towards the Col de la Colombière to Le Reposoir. Continue on the main road to Saint Bruno. Here, depending on the snow, it may be possible to drive up the track on the right to Malatrait.

Starting point	Saint Bruno
Starting altitude	1243m
Summit altitude	2098m
Altitude gain	855m
Time	5h round trip
Grade	2
Aspect	S, E
Map	1:25,000 IGN Top 25 3430 ET La Clusaz; 1:50,000 Didier Richard C Mont Blanc

range to the more distant glaciated peaks of the Mont Blanc chain, to the unmistakable Môle, to the far-off Lac Léman and the Jura beyond.

This walk is not long, but – in addition to its the stunning panorama – its main attraction is the terrain. Beginning in the forest the route emerges briefly at La Cha, to then return to the trees for a rising traverse that brings you out onto a delightful wide ridge, sparsely wooded and scattered with limestone boulders, that invites you to take a weaving route up past several false summits to the top.

Route

Take the track up past the gîte at Malatrait then continue in the forest to a clearing and the chalets at La Cha. Behind, there is an ascending path in the woods, which is signposted to the Tête des Bécus and La Forclaz. Follow this to a junction where a sign sends you left and up. Here it may be difficult to find the trail in the snow, although there are likely to be tracks or signs of one. There are occasional blue waymarks on the trees. The direction is north-east, and if you keep this direction you will reach the edge of the forest on a bouldery slope that takes you up to the rounded ridge and the Tête des Bécus. Views are spectacular in all directions. Head south-west along the broad ridge taking

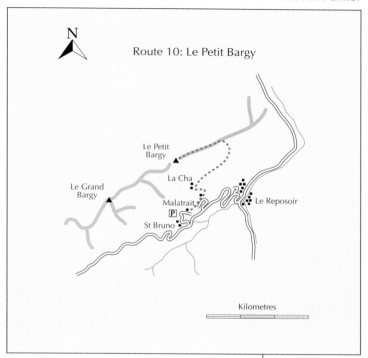

Route 10: Le Petit Bargy

the most attractive route. The summit is to be seen ahead, sporting a sign and a cross. Several false tops can be traversed or missed out as the mood takes you. Descend by the same route, with the option of a little variation along the ridge.

11: The Môle, 1863m

Access: From Cluses go to Bonneville then take the road to Faucigny and onwards to Saint Jean de Tholome. From here a small road leads to Bovère and then ends at Chez Béroud, where there is a good car park.

Starting point	Chez Béroud
Starting altitude	1127m
Summit altitude	1863m
Altitude gain	750m
Time	4h round trip
Grade	to Petit Môle 1, to Môle 3
Aspect	S, W
Map	1:25,000 IGN Top 25 3429 ET Bonneville-Cluses; 1:50,000 Didier Richard B Chablais Faucigny Genevois

Drive down the Arve valley from Chamonix towards Cluses, past the Aravis massif and the huge limestone cliffs flanking the valley, onwards towards Bonneville. This is the flatlands, the home of industrial estates. The mountains are just a snowy glimmer behind you when, all at once, looming up like a volcano in the middle of nowhere, is the Môle – isolated, ostracised by the rest of the mountains. This is a unique peak that cries out to be ascended, not only for the view, which is exceptional, but also for the interest of the ascent.

This is not an easy walk, however, there being considerable risks during certain snow conditions. Fortunately the Petit Môle (see 'Further options' below), which is really just a promontory on the southern shoulder of the Môle, provides an good alternative, to be considered when the snowpack is not stable.

From the Petit Môle views are excellent, stretching from the valley below and the mountains beyond – the Bargy massif, the Rochers de Leschaux, the Pointe de Sous Dine and the Sommet d'Andey – all the way to the Mont Blanc massif, the Aiguilles Rouges and Mont Buet.

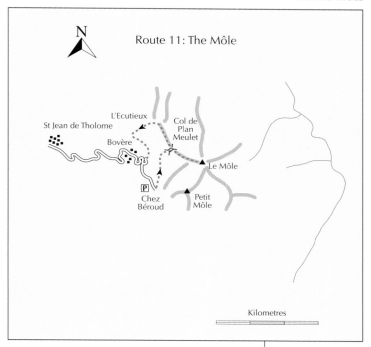

Route 11: The Môle

The Môle itself leaves little to the imagination, giving a stunning 360° panorama. This summit is really quite exposed – with sharp arêtes leading up on all sides. The drop-off is impressive, and you'll need to take a solid stance before allowing your gaze to fully concentrate on this fabulous vista. The Arve valley on the south side is complemented to the north by the less developed Giffre valley, with its villages and grey cliffs huddled amongst unspoilt greenery. As far as the eye can see are mountains – some snowy, some rocky, others green, with grey shadows outlined against glaciers behind.

Route

Take the track which goes north into the forest. After

The snowy cap of the Môle

Further Options

To reach the Petit Môle, 1534m, from Chez Béroud take the track into the forest as described above but take the second right turning which traverses up and across just under the chalets of La Lardère and the Petit Môle. Go up easily to these. Take a look at the orientation map then descend the same way.

some way there are a couple of junctions with paths going off to the right. Stay on the left, heading north and passing close to the high-tension cables. Eventually you go under the cables and follow the electricity line to come out of the forest at the col of Plan Meulet, 1563m, on the west ridge of the Môle, which is followed, rather steeply in places, to the summit.

To descend, retrace your steps as far as Plan Meulet, taking care down the ridge. Then continue along the arête over the small hill of Tête de L'Ecutieux, 1627m, and remain on the ridge until you reach the edge of the forest near the buildings of Ecutieux. Turn left here and pick up a track which descends in the forest. Don't follow this too far – at around 1200m you need to head left again to make a descending traverse to come out on the road near Bovère. Follow the road back to Chez Béroud.

12: Col de Coux, 1920m, and La Berte, 1992m

Starting point	L'Erigné
Starting altitude	1186m
Summit altitude	1992m
Altitude gain	806m
Time	4h30 round trip
Grade	2
Aspect	W
Map	1:25,000 IGN Top 25 3530 ET Samoëns; 1:50,000 Didier Richard B Chablais Faucigny Genevois

Access: From Morzine take the road up the Vallée de la Manche, which is also signed to the Nyons cable car. Park at the end of the road at the hamlet of L'Erigné.

As a relatively moderate route over to Switzerland the Col de Coux (or Cou) is steeped in history, and stories abound of smugglers sneaking over in the dead of night or thick fog laden with all manner of contraband goods, from tobacco to alcohol to meat, which was (and still is) much cheaper in France than in Switzerland.

La Berte is only a little higher than the col, but makes a great objective for a day walk. The route is not quite as easy as it appears on the map, as the slopes are steep in places, but the difficulty is never too great and the views well worth it. If you have two cars you could continue on over and finish up in Champèry, but for most people this will be a circuit. Views of the Dents du Midi and Dents Blanches are fabulous.

Route

From L'Erigné follow the track into the forest to the chalets of Le Charny, and continue on up to the Mines d'Or lake and the Freterolles chalets beyond. Head directly east, more or less following the Freterolles stream-bed to the Col de Coux, 1920m. Above is La Berte, easily ascended by its north ridge.

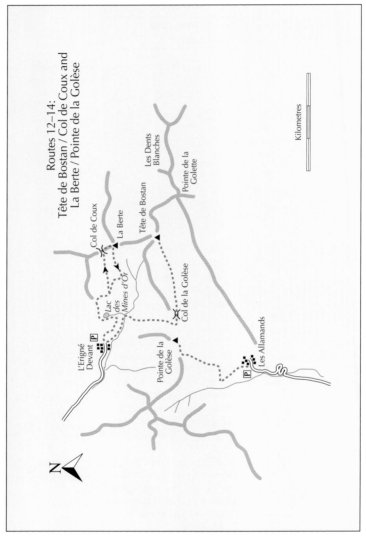

Routes 12–14:
Tête de Bostan / Col de Coux and
La Berte / Pointe de la Golèse

Les Dents Blanches

Pointe de la Golette

Col de Coux

La Berte

Tête de Bostan

Col de la Golèse

Lac des Mines d'Or

L'Erigné Devant

Pointe de la Golèse

Les Allamands

N

Kilometres

Descend either back the same way or, for a circuit, descend by the west ridge to the edge of the forest. Here pick up the GR5 summer path, which is well signed with red and white flashes, usually visible in the trees. Follow this around to the Chardonnière chalets at 1346m then return to Le Charny and L'Erigné by the snowed-up track.

13: Tête de Bostan, 2406m

Starting point	L'Erigné
Starting altitude	1186m
Summit altitude	2406m
Altitude gain	1220m from L'Erigné
Time	6–7h round trip
Grade	2
Aspect	N, W
Map	1:25,000 IGN Top 25 3530 ET Samoëns; 1:50,000 Didier Richard B Chablais Faucigny Genevois

Access: From Morzine take the road up the Vallée de la Manche, which is also signed to the Nyons cable car. Park at the end of the road at the hamlet of Erigné.

'Bostan', sometimes written as 'Bossetan', is local dialect for 'valley of cows', but that would be to underestimate this fine summit, which provides a splendid panorama of high peaks – the Dents Blanches, Dents de Midi and, almost hiding in the background, Mont Blanc. The Tête de Bostan is a very popular objective in the winter, not only because of its views but also because it is accessible from two main resorts, Samoëns and Morzine. There's not a lot of difference in difficulty between the two routes; the Samoëns approach is described in 'Further Options' on p.110.

The walk is interesting from both sides, and the routes converge at the Col de la Golèse. This pass is famous as a migratory passage for birds, although you're unlikely to see many when you're on snowshoes – they should already have reached their destination.

The Tête de Bostan in lean conditions

Further Options The Col de la Golèse can be reached from Samoëns. Drive up towards Les Allamands and park before the hamlet at the car park at pt 997m. The Col de la Golèse is reached from Les Allamands by following the true left bank of the Crêt stream to the Chalet de Crêt Vosy. From here a northerly line through the forest brings you out onto the summer road. This continues to Les Bois, from where you take a south-westerly route to the col.

The walk is interesting and quite long, giving a good day out with no technical difficulty.

Route

From L'Erigné follow the track into the forest to the chalets of Le Charny. At the last chalet take the flat forest track to the right alongside the stream. This comes out at a bridge and signpost, where you go right following a wide track up to the Refuge de Vigny. Above is the Col de la Golèse, where there is another refuge.

From the col head up and around to the south on the slopes of L'Avouille. At around 2000m join the rounded ridge and continue past a false summit to the final slightly steeper slopes and the true summit of the Tête de Bostan.

Descend by the same route, varying the upper slopes down to the col according to the snow.

14: Pointe de la Golèse, 1835m

Slightly less well-known than its neighbour the Tête de Bostan, the Pointe de la Golèse consequently enjoys a

Starting point	Les Allamands
Starting altitude	997m
Summit altitude	1835m
Altitude gain	838m
Time	4h30
Grade	2
Aspect	S
Map	1:25,000 IGN Top 25 3530 ET Samoëns; 1:50,000 Didier Richard 3 Chablais Faucigny Genevois

Access: From Cluses drive up to Taninges then along to Samoëns. Go through the village past Les Moulins and continue on this small road to Les Allamands. Park just before the houses.

little more solitude, yet provides equally good views. The route can be undertaken from Morzine or, as described here, from Samoëns.

Whilst this walk is not particularly long, it does require a knowledge of route-finding to choose the best way up undulating slopes under the summit. The south slopes of the Pointe de la Golèse can present a risk of avalanche, under which circumstances this peak should not be considered.

From the top you'll have good views down to the Col de la Golèse, with its refuge (closed in winter), and of the long whaleback ridge of the Tête de Bossetan. To the south-west are the rocky peaks of the Aravis and Bargy ranges.

Route

From the parking area at Les Allamands take the track which goes north into the sparse forest alongside the stream to the chalet Cret Vosy. Continue directly to the north to pick up a forest track, which is taken to Les Chavonnes then along east to Les Bois (Les Chavonnes can be missed out by cutting up direct). Follow a track, if it's visible, above the tree-line until level with the Chalet de la Croix at 1500m, then go up the slopes above heading north. Initially quite steep, the terrain eases at Les Cramots. Above, the south-west ridge of the Pointe de la Golèse is obvious. There is a slight dip in the ridge (1770m), which you need to gain by taking the easiest line up the slopes before following the arête eastwards to the summit. Descend by the same route.

15: Fer à Cheval, 1012m

Access: From Samoëns drive along the Giffre valley to Sixt Fer à Cheval, then continue alongside the river to the end of the road at Plan des Lacs.

Starting point	Plan des Lacs
Starting altitude	955m
Summit altitude	1012m
Altitude gain	150m
Time	2h30 round trip
Grade	1
Aspect	N
Map	1:25,000 IGN Top 25 3530 ET Samoëns; 1:50,000 Didier Richard B Chablais Faucigny Genevois
Public transport	Bus Samoëns–Sixt–Plan des Lacs

The Fer à Cheval, near the village of Sixt Fer à Cheval, is a spectacular cirque of huge cliffs and waterfalls, frozen in winter into curtains and daggers of ice. It is a cold and enclosed place – the trees blanketed in snow, the cliffs impregnable. There is no way through here, no summits to be climbed on snowshoes, but a stroll into this area is not to be missed in the depths of winter, when the fresh snow will be criss-crossed with animal tracks and the world enveloped in muffled silence.

This is also a paradise for cross-country skiers, but it is easy to avoid the pistes and to escape into a solitary world where the only sound will be the crunch of your snowshoes. You can wander where you wish, as long as you keep away from the steep walls of the cirque and the slopes along the Giffre river.

Route
Head back down the road to a bridge at pt 871. Leave the road here on the track heading south towards Les

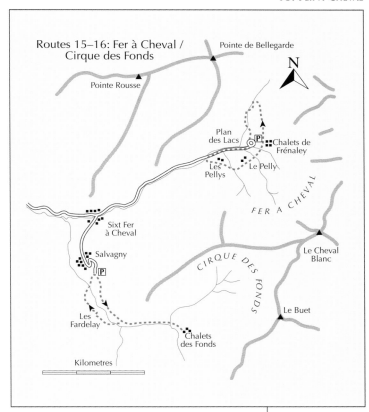

Routes 15–16: Fer à Cheval / Cirque des Fonds

Pointe de Bellegarde

Pointe Rousse

Plan des Lacs

Chalets de Frénaley

Les Pellys

Le Pelly

FER À CHEVAL

Sixt Fer à Cheval

Salvagny

Le Cheval Blanc

CIRQUE DES FONDS

Les Fardelay

Chalets des Fonds

Le Buet

Kilometres

Pellys, but almost immediately head uphill into the forest. Take a diagonal line south-east to meet the Nant de Combe Salliet and cross this stream at pt 1014. There is a path, but leave this to descend to the houses of Le Pelly. From here go north-east to cross two streams (Nant des Pères and Nant des Joathons) to arrive at the Chalets de Frénaley. Take a slightly descending traverse north through the forest until you arrive at the cross-country ski track. You can then walk alongside this to

The Col de la Golèse
with its refuge
(Route 14)

the bridge over the Giffre river at pt 1012. Return on the other side of the river. Throughout, views of the Fer à Cheval are magnificent.

16: Cirque des Fonds, 1368m

Access: From Samoëns drive along the Giffre valley to Sixt Fer à Cheval then turn right in the village and park in the hamlet of Salvagny.

Starting point	Salvagny
Starting altitude	870m
Summit altitude	1368m
Altitude gain	498m
Time	3h30 round trip
Grade	1
Aspect	W
Map	1:25,000 IGN Top 25 3530 ET Samoëns; 1:50,000 Didier Richard B Chablais Faucigny Genevois
Public transport	Bus Samoëns–Sixt–Salvagny

Similar to the Fer à Cheval but even wilder, the Cirque des Fonds (or Fonts on the latest 1:25,000 map) is only accessible on foot, so it is less frequented than its more famous neighbour. The cirque is partly formed by the west face of Mont Buet, composed of deep chimneys and dark forbidding buttresses. The Refuge des Fonds is only open in summer, but nevertheless the little group of chalets here makes a good objective for this walk, the aim being to venture into this intriguing and beautiful area.

Cooling off!

Route

At the chapel in the village take the forest track which goes towards Les Fonds. At a junction at pt 1072 do not turn left but remain on the main trail, past the chalet at La Celière, following the river with increasingly steep slopes on the left (north) side. At pt 1278 a bridge takes you over the Torrent des Fonds, and soon after you'll arrive at the Chalets des Fonds and the refuge. Above to the south you'll be able to make out the Petit Col d'Anterne, which gives access to the Plateau d'Anterne. Whilst this can be done on snowshoes, it is often dangerous because of the risk of avalanches. Enjoy splendid views of the impressive Cirque des Fonds from here.

To descend, return as far as La Celière then take the left-hand path which is signposted. Go down into the clearing at Le Pelly de Serai and onwards to the road at Les Fardelay. Opposite is the Cascade de Rouget, huge in the summer but usually frozen in winter. Take the GR5 footpath that cuts the road heading down (north) and back to Salvagny.

17: Tête de Moëde, 2459m

Access: From Sallanches take the road up to Passy then on to the Plateau d'Assy. Continue to the end of the road at the ski resort of Plaine Joux.

Starting point	Plaine Joux
Starting altitude	1337m
Summit altitude	Col d'Anterne 2257m, Tête de Moëde 2459m
Altitude gain	920m for the Col d'Anterne, 1122m for the Tête de Moëde
Time	3h30–4h to the col, 5h to the summit. 2–3h for the descent.
Grade	3
Aspect	S, W
Map	1:25,000 IGN Top 25 3530 ET Samoëns; 1:50,000 Didier Richard C Mont Blanc
Public transport	Bus Sallanches–Plaine Joux
Accommodation	It may be possible to get into the highest chalet at the Chalets de Moëde, just south-east from the Refuge. However, this is not a hut and is not equipped.

Sometimes it is said that there is no wilderness in the Alps any more. This may be true around some of the ski resorts, but wild places do remain, and this is one of them. Although not far from the lifts of Chamonix or Plaine Joux, the Tête de Moëde feels quite remote and serious. There are other possibilities in this area, noted below, and none of them should be underestimated.

Access is long and there are significant dangers of avalanches along much of the route. Although there is a mountain hut nearby, this is closed in winter, so you must choose your day and be sure to start early and to adjust your objectives if necessary. That said, the Tête de Moëde or the nearer Col d'Anterne make for a great walk. Much of the ascent takes place beneath the impressively over-

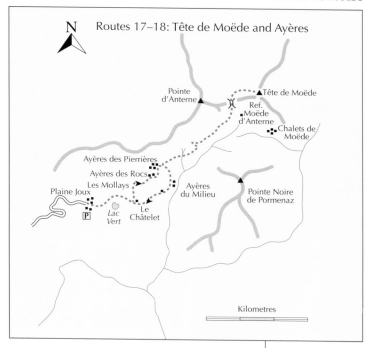

Routes 17–18: Tête de Moëde and Ayères

N

hanging cliffs of the Rochers des Fiz and d'Anterne. With fabulous views of Mont Blanc to the south you will be on visual overload. Once at the summit you are confronted with the appealing Plateau d'Anterne, which just begs for you to have the time to visit, but it is extremely unlikely that in a day you could also do justice to this remote spot. Views extend down to the Arve valley below and to the Aravis range beyond. The north-east is dominated by the huge snowy summit of Mont Buet.

This is a place to visit when you want to really get away from it all. However, don't expect to be alone: despite its challenge this walk attracts plenty of snow-shoers and skiers alike, but you can be sure they will all be equally appreciative of the scenery.

The Tête de Moëde is a superb vantage point

Route

From Plaine Joux traverse under the ski pistes and follow the snowy, relatively flat road, staying above Lac Vert, to Le Châtelet. Head up to the attractive hamlet of Les Mollays then on to Ayères des Rocs and Ayères des Pierrières. Remember to look behind you – the view is already superb.

From here the route takes a very long rising traverse under worryingly steep slopes. If it is hot, or if there has been fresh snowfall, and these slopes have not yet avalanched you are not advised to continue. You are following a summer track which is waymarked red and white, but you may not see these flashes. There will, however, be tracks of skis and snowshoes in good conditions. It is sometimes possible to take the bed of the Souay torrent, but this is only practicable in certain conditions and is best avoided.

After interminable traversing you'll arrive at the Refuge du Col d'Anterne, also known as the Refuge de Moëde d'Anterne. The Col d'Anterne is above, accessed by quite steep slopes which tend to get a lot of sun, and therefore the snow gets wet and heavy during the day.

When you arrive at the col look at your watch. If it is after midday you would be advised to call it a day here. Otherwise continue along the ridge all the way up to the Tête de Moëde. Descend by the same route.

Further Options Possibilities abound. The Pointe Noire de Pormenaz presents an obvious challenge, being situated right opposite the Tête de Moëde, towering above the Gorges de la Diosaz. This is reached from the Refuge d'Anterne by its north slopes. A more modest objective would be pt 2033, just south of the refuge. This forms a fine viewpoint and is easily reached after the long traverse.

Whatever you choose to do, do not attempt to descend the Gorges de la Diosaz, as this is not possible.

18: Ayères, 1641m

Starting point	Plaine Joux
Starting altitude	1337m
Summit altitude	1641m
Altitude gain	304m
Time	3h round trip
Grade	1
Aspect	S
Map	1:25,000 IGN Top 25 3530 ET Samoëns; 1:50,000 Didier Richard C Mont Blanc
Public transport	Bus Sallanches–Plaine Joux

Access: From Sallanches take the road up to Passy then on to the Plateau d'Assy. Continue to the end of the road at the ski resort of Plaine Joux.

If you're dreaming of a nice gentle walk, with views worthy of a major peak, then this one is for you. In one direction are the snowy glaciated peaks of the Mont Blanc massif, with its eponymous summit as the centre-piece, and in the other huge soaring golden cliffs set against an azure sky. Varied and interesting terrain completes this idyllic gem.

The hamlet of Ayères, with Mont Blanc behind

The ski resort of Plaine Joux provides the access point, but you are soon away from the lifts and skiers and enjoying forests and summer alpages at their best. Take a special picnic and while away a day immersed in this paradise. Once you reach the hamlets of Ayères don't be tempted to go up close to the steep slopes under the cliffs above as there is a high risk of avalanches here.

Route

From Plaine Joux traverse under the ski pistes and follow the snowy, relatively flat road, staying above Lac Vert, to Le Châtelet. Head straight up in the forest to the attractive hamlet of Les Mollays, and then on to Ayères des Rocs and Ayères des Pierrières.

Beyond the chalets descend directly to the chalets of Ayères du Milieu or by a summer track to Souay then round to Ayères du Milieu. Follow the track to Le Gouet then Le Châtelet to return to Plaine Joux.

CHAMONIX REGION

Chamonix

There are various places to stay in the Chamonix valley. Chamonix itself is an interesting town, very busy in the high season, but there is plenty going on and it has a wide range of facilities. However, there are not many possibilities for snowshoe walks leaving immediately from the town.

Les Houches

At the far south end of the Chamonix valley, Les Houches is a popular town with all facilities. It is well placed for getting to the walks further away in the Aravis and Beaufortain range, although a little far from Switzerland. The Mont Blanc tunnel makes it convenient for Italy too. However, it is a skiers' town, and the streets can be very busy in the holidays.

Argentière

Conveniently situated just 8km from Chamonix, Argentière combines some of the advantages of the tourist town with the atmosphere of a smaller village, albeit a very lively one at some times of the day. There are plenty of places to stay and to eat, and the train and bus services are frequent.

Vallorcine

Situated to the north of the Chamonix valley, Vallorcine is a different world from the hustle and bustle of the main tourist area. The Col des Montets divides the valley from that of Chamonix and Argentière, and in winter there are usually several days when the col is closed because of the risk of avalanches. Nowadays, the problem of access to Vallorcine is more or less resolved by the railway that runs from Chamonix to Martigny, via a tunnel through the col, and provides almost certain access. Cars can also drive through the railway tunnel – when there's no train of course!

Vallorcine is a small, quiet village with few shops and bars. It is an ideal base for snowshoeing, as you can walk out of the door and set off. Most hillsides are still free of ski lifts, and here you'll find the true winter experience.

19: Le Prarion, 1969m

Access: From
Chamonix head
down the valley to
Les Houches. At the
far (west) end of the
town, just after the
Prarion cable-car sta-
tion, take the road
up to Les Chavants
and continue to park
at La Côte.

Starting point	La Côte
Starting altitude	1131m
Summit altitude	1969m
Altitude gain	838m
Time	4h30–5h round trip
Grade	1
Aspect	E, N
Map	1:25,000 IGN Top 25 3531 ET St-Gervais-les-Bains; 1:50,000 Didier Richard C Mont Blanc
Public transport	Bus/train Chamonix–Les Houches

Les Houches, at the western end of the Chamonix valley,
benefits from relatively safe slopes as much of it is heavily wooded. It is also conveniently placed next to Mont
Blanc, so of course views are superb. This walk ascends
in the woods, taking in the Tête Noire, before coming
out above the tree-line at Le Prarion, from where the
panorama is quite splendid, ranging from the Mont
Blanc and its associated peaks to the far-off Col de
Balme, forming the Franco-Swiss border at the head of
the valley, and the sunny southern slopes of the Aiguilles
Rouges massif, flanking the valley's eastern side. Whilst
very close to the ski area of Les Houches, you generally
will not be aware of the nearby skiiers on this quiet walk.

Route
From La Côte follow the track up to the attractive old
chalets at Charousse, used as the location for several
films. From here take a zigzag path up in the forest to the
Col de la Forclaz. A good detour here is the Tête Noire,
straight above to the north-east. Through the trees you'll
enjoy views of the nearby massif.
Return to the Col de la Forclaz and take the steepish

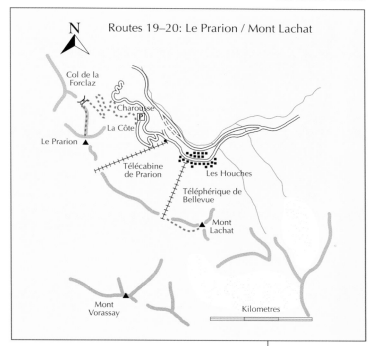

Routes 19–20: Le Prarion / Mont Lachat

N

Col de la Forclaz

Charousse

P

La Côte

Le Prarion ▲

Télécabine de Prarion

Les Houches

Téléphérique de Bellevue

▲ Mont Lachat

Mont Vorassay ▲

Kilometres

ridge south, emerging from the trees at Le Prarion. Any further and you'll get embroiled with the skiers. Take the time to stand and stare at the wonderful panorama spread out in front of you. Descend by the same route.

20: Mont Lachat, 2115m

This is a real quickie, reserved for a lazy day when you've enjoyed a *grasse matinée*, as the French so delightfully describe a lie-in. It is really just a higher viewpoint than you would get from the Les Houches cable car, but still worth doing for a first day, or when you just want to take photos, sit in the sun and enjoy the splendour of the Chamonix peaks.

Further Options It is possible to reach the Col de la Forclaz from St Gervais via Montfort and Le Pontet.

Access: From Chamonix head down the valley to Les Houches. The Bellevue lift station is to be found about halfway through town.

Starting point	Summit of the Bellevue lift station
Starting altitude	1801m
Summit altitude	2115m
Altitude gain	314m
Time	1h30 round trip
Grade	1
Aspect	NW
Map	1:25,000 IGN Top 25 3531 ET St-Gervais-les-Bains; 1:50,000 Didier Richard C Mont Blanc
Public transport	Bus/train service Chamonix–Les Houches

Route
Climb the obvious summit of Mont Lachat to the south-west of the lift station. Don't go too far or you'll end up on the Aiguille du Goûter! Descend by the same route.

21: Pointe Helbronner, 3462m, to Aiguille du Midi, 3842m

Access: From Courmayeur drive up to La Palud and the Helbronner cable car. Take cars for the three stages to the top.

Starting point	Pointe Helbronner
Starting altitude	3462m
Summit altitude	3842m
Altitude gain	650m
Time	4h
Grade	G4
Aspect	N, S
Map	1:25,000 IGN Top 25 3531 ET St-Gervais-les-Bains; 1:50,000 Didier Richard C Mont Blanc
Public transport	Bus Aosta–Courmayeur–La Palud

There can be no finer mountain setting than the Glacier du Géant. Whether gained from Italy or France, cable cars give instant high altitude access to a wonderland of gleaming snowy summits, golden rock faces and soaring spires.

This is a world of sweeping glaciers and deep, gaping crevasses, vertical pillars and poised boulders to take your breath away. Yet this magical, spectacular world is also accessible on snowshoes, as long as you are suitably experienced and equipped for a glacier walk.

Whether accessed from Courmayeur or Chamonix, the walk between Pointe Helbronner and the Aiguille du Midi will be equally memorable. It is described below from Italy, as there tend to be fewer people coming up from the Italian side, it is easier to see the best line up the Glacier du Géant when ascending, and it is probably less frightening to climb up the final arête to the Aiguille du Midi – with its precipitous drop down to the Chamonix valley – after several hours of walking rather than first thing in the morning.

This walk is in a league of its own, one to save for a very special day and one to savour. Leave plenty of time,

Looking into Italy from the Col d'Entrèves (photo: Francine Pasche)

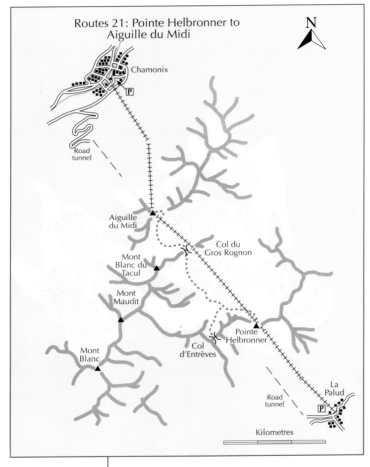

Routes 21: Pointe Helbronner to Aiguille du Midi

N

Chamonix

P

Road tunnel

Aiguille du Midi

Col du Gros Rognon

Mont Blanc du Tacul

Mont Maudit

Mont Blanc

Col d'Entrèves

Pointe Helbronner

La Palud

P

Road tunnel

Kilometres

first for a cappuccino on the viewing platform of Pointe Helbronner way above Courmayeur, then to be awed by the icy scenery and the impressive buttresses and gullies of Mont Blanc du Tacul, and finally for the breathless finale up the arête.

After checking out the Aiguille du Midi take the cherry-like gondolas to return to the Helbronner lift and down to La Palud.

Route

From the tiny third lift follow the corridor to a door that leads out onto a walkway and then the top of a slope. The cables of the car that will bring you back after the walk are just above. Rope up, then walk underneath these cables and over the Col des Flambeaux. From here take the least-crevassed way down north-west, past the Aiguille du Toule on the left, to the relative flat of the junction between the Glacier du Géant and the unnamed glacier that descends from the Cirque Maudit to the west. There is an obviously crevassed area here, and this can be largely avoided by keeping below it. Then take the gently ascending slopes of the Glacier du Géant north-north-west under the east faces of Pointe Adolphe Rey, the Pyramide de Tacul, Mont Blanc du Tacul and the Pointe Lachenal. After the Col du Gros Rognon the slope becomes almost flat for a while. Ahead is the attractive golden rocky south face of the Aiguille du Midi. Follow the glacier under this and up to the steepening that leads up rightwards onto the col under the east ridge of the Aiguille du Midi. Shorten the rope and follow the deep trench in the arête that leads up to the entrance to the cable car.

The Aiguille Noire, Aiguille Blanche and Mont Blanc de Courmayeur

Further Options

From Helbronner an equally good choice is to go to the Col d'Entrèves, 3527m. Follow the route described as far as the base of the Aiguille du Toule. Turn left and ascend the gradually steepening glacier which goes between the east face of the Tour Ronde and the west face of the Aiguille d'Entrèves. As the glacier flattens at 3500m the Col d'Entrèves is directly ahead. It is worth going up to a *brèche* just on the right of the col for fabulous views of the Peutrey ridge, formed by the Aiguille Noire, the Aiguille Blanche and, in between, the spiky Dames Anglaises and the Val Vény far, far below. Descend by the same route and retrace your steps back up to Helbronner.

22: Aiguillette des Houches, 2285m

Access: From the church in Chamonix head uphill to the Brévent lift station. Take the gondola lift to Plan Praz then the cable car to Le Brévent.

Starting point	Le Brévent
Starting altitude	2525m
Summit altitude	2285m
Altitude gain	185m plus 400m for the return to Le Brévent
Time	5h round trip: 2h30 to the summit – can be longer if the descent is difficult – and 2h30 for the return
Grade	3
Aspect	W, N (S)
Map	1:25,000 IGN Top 25 3531 ET St-Gervais-les-Bains
Public transport	Train Les Houches–Chamonix if you descend by the south face to Le Coupeau

Whilst not a major summit compared to the giants all around, the Aiguillette des Houches provides unbeatable views of the neighbouring glaciated peaks. Situated at the southern end of the Aiguilles Rouges range, right opposite the Mont Blanc massif, the Aiguillette des Houches occupies a privileged position. Indeed, it was from Le Brévent, the access point for this route, that in 1760 the young Genevan botanist Horace Bénédict de Saussure came up with the then innovatory idea that he'd like to climb to the summit of Mont Blanc. It was to be another 26 years before Jacques Balmat and Gabriel Paccard succeeded in this feat (see 'Mont Blanc', p.18), but it is a testimony to the magnificent view of the peak when seen from this vantage point that de Saussure was so inspired.

Accessible from the Brévent cable car, the Aiguillette des Houches summit is a popular outing. However, beware – snow conditions can render the initial descent

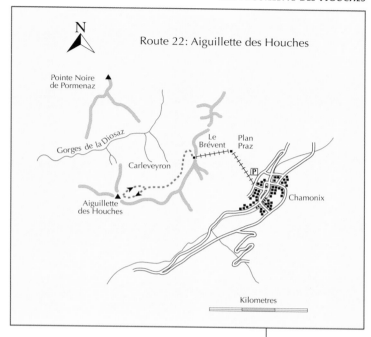

Route 22: Aiguillette des Houches

from the ski pistes quite demanding. It is possible from the summit to descend the southern slopes to the village of Le Coupeau, but this can often be dangerous in the heat of the afternoon as these slopes are quite steep. Unless you are sure about the conditions it is much better to plan to return to the Brévent cable car, but it is essential to allow sufficient time for the 400m climb back up, which can be a sweaty experience to say the least. It would not be good to miss the last lift down after all that effort!

Route
The route begins with the descent from Le Brévent. Follow the ski piste (staying well to the side) until the first bend then duck under the rope at the edge of the piste.

Going back up to the Brévent with the Aiguillette des Houches in the background

The route for the descent will be dictated by the snow conditions and your ease on steep ground. This descent should not be underestimated – it is this that gives the grade 3 to this route. The terrain is composed of hills and drop-offs, and route-finding skills are useful here. In bad visibility this peak should not be undertaken. The easiest line is to head diagonally left (east) down the south-west slope under the lift station, staying above the Creux aux Marmottes, to join the Grand Balcon path before the Tête de Bellachat. The summer path can the often be followed from here down to the Col de Bellachat, 2130m. However, common sense must be used to find the easiest way through – beware of icy patches and avalanche risk.

From a low point of about 2100m the ascent takes gentle terrain in a generally west-south-west direction. The route can be made more interesting by using natural features to create a smooth and curving track up to the summit; look carefully at the map – the Aiguillette des Houches is actually the west-most summit on the ridge.

The descent is usually a delight, as these north-facing slopes hold cold powder-snow long after the last snowfall. Take whichever line appeals, being sure to head across right (east) to the point where you started ascending the summit. Do not be tempted to head north into the Gorges de la Diosaz – there is no descent route this way.

From 2100m it is best more or less to follow your descent route back up to Le Brévent. These slopes will be much hotter than when you descended, so watch out for wet snow slides. Be sure to have plenty of drink left for this section, as it gets extremely hot sometimes. The last lift down is usually around 4.30pm, but check this before you set off.

Those who choose to descend from the summit to Le Coupeau should take the steep south-facing slope to the edge of the forest, where the summer path in the trees can be picked up and followed to Le Coupeau. From here head down the road to the train station of Les Houches and catch the train back to Chamonix.

23: Col de Bérard, 2460m

Starting point	Le Buet
Starting altitude	1329m
Summit altitude	2460m
Altitude gain	1131m
Time	6h round trip
Grade	2
Aspect	NE
Map	1:25,000 IGN Top 25 3630 OT Chamonix; 1:50,000 Didier Richard C Mont Blanc
Public transport	Train Vallorcine–Le Buet–Chamonix

Access: From Chamonix take the train or drive to Le Buet. There's a big car park at the station, opposite the Hotel du Buet.

The Bérard valley is one of the gems of the area. Although it does get a lot of ski traffic from ski tourers

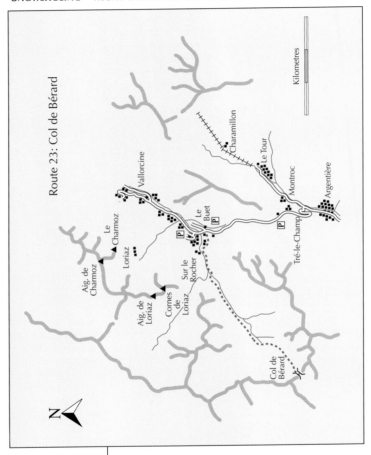

Route 23: Col de Bérard

who come over from the Chamonix ski areas, it is still a magical place. Early in the morning it is cold and shady, and you'll find animal tracks on the slopes above. As the sun starts to rise you can watch its golden rays touch the summits of Mont Oreb and the Cornes de Loriaz as you ascend.

The Col de Bérard provides a fantastic belvedere: you'll be greeted with views of the Rochers des Fiz, the Pointe Noire de Pormenaz and away down to the Arve valley and beyond. Don't be surprised to meet lots of people here, especially on sunny weekends.

Coming down you'll be able to stay away from the skiers by picking a different line to descend. Later, stay on the true left side of the valley as far as the bridge described in the ascent.

Resting after the long climb up to the Col de Bérard

Route

From the Hotel du Buet head up towards the Bérard valley, passing the cluster of houses near the ski pistes then following the signs to the *cascade* until you are in the valley. Follow the true right side of the river past one bridge to the cascade café (shut in winter) and a second signed to Tré les Eaux. At the third bridge over the river you have a choice. Remain on the true right bank, following the ski tracks, which can be icy in places, or, usually better, you can cross over and go along the left bank.

At about 1600m the terrain flattens out for a while. Take the right side of the river and follow the valley up to

133

The pleasant slopes down from the Col de Bérard – we weren't the first here!

the steepening at about 1900m. The Refuge de Pierre à Bérard is here, but is usually buried under snow. Head south towards the Combe de Bérard and then south-west up the cwm to the obvious Col de Bérard. The terrain is rolling, so search around to find the easiest and most pleasant line. Descend by the same route.

24: Mont Buet, 3096m

Le Buet (also known as Mont Buet to distinguish it from the nearby village of the same name) is commonly know as Le Mont Blanc des Dames ('the ladies' Mont Blanc'), presumably because it is considerably lower than Mont Blanc and can be done as a training peak before going on to loftier summits. However, it is a summit that must not be underestimated: it is considered a long undertaking in summer, let alone in winter, when the snow and weather conditions can make it a serious challenge.

The best snow conditions for snowshoeing Mont Buet are likely to be encountered in January and

Starting point	Le Buet
Starting altitude	1329m
Summit altitude	3096m
Altitude gain	1767m
Time	8–10h round trip
Grade	3
Aspect	E, S
Map	1:25,000 IGN Top 25 3630 OT Chamonix; 1:50,000 Didier Richard C Mont Blanc
Public transport	Train Vallorcine–Le Buet–Chamonix

Access: From Chamonix take the train or drive to Le Buet. There's a big car park at the station, opposite the Hotel du Buet.

February, when the slopes don't receive too much sun and consequently are not too icy in the mornings; but at this time of year the days are short and cold, and this is a long walk. Later, in March and April, conditions can be good, but certain slopes may be icy, so it can be a good precaution to take along crampons too, just in case.

Despite its length, and the possibility of difficult snow conditions, plus the fact that this summit is also popular with skiers, Mont Buet is one of the major snow-shoe summits and provides an unforgettable ascent. The Bérard valley, used to access the peak, is beautiful, and the summit views of the Mont Blanc massif, the Aravis and the Valais mountains are truly spectacular.

The route is very long and requires an early start and a certain level of fitness and preparation. The final slopes are difficult and tiring unless you are experienced in the techniques of climbing and traversing steep ground.

This is a summit only to be attempted when you've got plenty of other snowshoe summits under your belt, when the snow cover is plentiful but the avalanche risk is not too high, when it's not too hot, and when you are feeling well rested and in need of a really hard day!

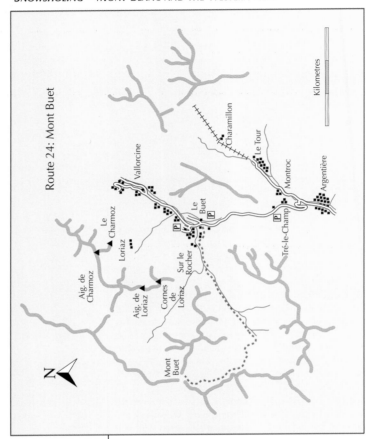

Route 24: Mont Buet

Kilometres

Charamillon

Le Tour

Vallorcine

Montroc

Argentière

Le Charmoz

Le Buet

Loriaz

Tré-le-Champ

Sur le Rocher

Aig. de Charmoz

Aig. de Loriaz

Cornes de Loriaz

Mont Buet

N

Route

From the Hotel du Buet head up towards the Bérard valley, passing the cluster of houses near the ski pistes then
following the signs to the *cascade* until you're in the valley. Follow the true right side of the river past one bridge
to the cascade café (shut in winter) and a second signed
to Tré les Eaux. At the third bridge over the river there is a

choice. Remain on the true right bank, following the ski tracks, which can be icy in places, or cross over and go along the left bank – this will be less icy but you might have to make the track, which can be hard work.

At about 1600m the terrain flattens out for a while. It is best to get onto the right bank of the river here before the steepening which leads to the initial slopes of Mont Buet. You'll pass close to the tiny Refuge de Pierre à Bérard, but probably won't see it as it is well hidden by a boulder and almost always buried in winter. From about 1925m the route heads towards the Col de Salenton before skirting around under the Aiguille de Salenton. There is some avalanche risk here, especially later in the day when the slopes above get heated up – so don't linger.

A long traverse brings you to 2650m, under the final slopes. If it is late or you are tired at this point it is best to turn around – you've already had great views and it is a long way back down. The last 450m are steep and

A solitary person ascends Mont Buet above a sea of cloud

consequently quite arduous. Take the easiest line up the slope above before heading north to hit the Arête de La Mortine to the north of the radio mast. Follow the rounded ridge to the summit cairn.

Descend by more or less the same route. Whilst in good snow you'll be able to take a direct line down some of the higher slopes, be careful not to descend too low before traversing under the Aiguille de Salenton – you may see ski tracks descending directly south, but it is difficult and steep ground, and it is easy to get stuck in the gully leading down from the Creux aux Vaches. Follow the Bérard valley back to Le Buet, dodging out of the way periodically as skiers scrape past you on the narrow track, and go celebrate in the hotel bar.

25: Bérard Valley and Sur le Rocher, 1530m

Access: From Chamonix drive or take the train to the hamlet of Le Buet.

Starting point	Le Buet
Starting altitude	1329m
Summit altitude	1560m
Altitude gain	231m
Time	2h–2h30 round trip
Grade	1
Aspect	N, S
Map	1:25,000 IGN Top 25 3630 OT Chamonix; 1:50,000 Didier Richard C Mont Blanc
Public transport	Train Vallorcine–Le Buet–Chamonix

In the summer the Bérard valley is teeming with people, some walking up to the Refuge Pierre à Bérard, some climbing Mont Buet, and others just enjoying the sun and the river. In winter it's a different story – on a sunny day there will be lots of skiers and snowshoers in the valley, but pick a day after fresh snow, in the morning, and you may well be making fresh tracks. This is

Heading to Sur le Rocher the morning after fresh snow

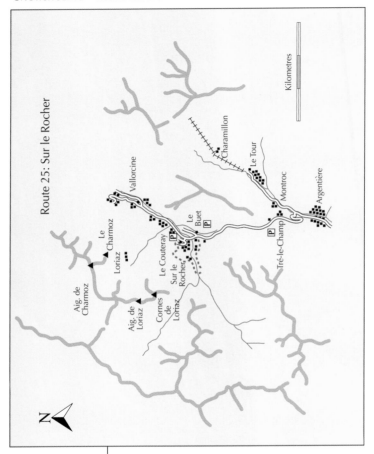

Route 25: Sur le Rocher

certainly the very best time to explore the Bérard, when no one else is around, the trees are heavy with a blanket of powder, and animal tracks decorate the boulders of the river bed.

However, even if you do this walk on a busy holiday afternoon, the beauty of the valley will not escape you.

The Bérard river may be frozen or just partly so, the boulders are usually loaded high with the season's snowfall, and way above are impressive rocky summits, shining in the golden winter sunlight. This early section of the walk is to be savoured.

After half an hour or so the valley is left to traverse round to the summer hamlet of Sur Le Rocher, a perfect picnic site, from where the Aiguille Verte can be glimpsed through the trees. Continue onwards towards the far less-frequented Tré les Eaux valley, which is then left to emerge from the trees at Les Granges, another hamlet of summer houses, many of them very old traditional buildings. From here it's a short walk down to the starting point, Le Buet.

This relatively short walk provides a perfect introductory day, an outing to find your legs at the start of the holiday, or simply the opportunity to linger among the trees, at the river's edge, or on the sunny balcony of a wooden chalet, taking in the pleasures of winter in the Alps.

Route

From the Hotel du Buet head up towards the ski lifts of La Poya, but keep away from the skiers by heading directly for the cluster of houses up on the right of the pistes (this tiny ski area is generally used by children and beginners, so don't expect skiers to be able to avoid you if you get in their way). From the houses go straight up (east) and you'll be channelled into the Bérard valley – there are signs for the *cascade*. Once in the valley just follow the river. The track usually stays just above the river bed, although when there's plenty of snow it is possible to weave about among the boulders of the river. Avoid getting wet, however, as not only is this cold but any water on your snowshoes will freeze and leave you with icy lumps to drag along.

In good weather, after about midday, this valley sees a fair number of ski tourers descending having skied over from the Chamonix valley. It is advisable, therefore, to avoid being here in the afternoon; otherwise, be careful on bends where you can't be seen, as some skiers come down very fast.

Cross the first wooden bridge over the river, signed to Tré les Eaux, and head back along the other side of the river, the true left bank, taking a rising traverse – the summer path may or may not be visible here, but you need to ascend diagonally to come out at Sur Le Rocher. It can be difficult to find the precise way, but there are red flashes at times on trees, and if you keep going north-east you'll finally find the hamlet at 1534m.

Be aware throughout the section in the valley that there are steep slopes above, and when the avalanche risk is high this is not a good place to be. Even though there are trees, this is no guarantee that snow slides will not occur.

A sign indicates the direction to Tré les Eaux. This quickly brings you to a beautiful large flat clearing with great views of Mont Oreb and the Cornes de Loriaz. On the right, in the trees, is the way to Les Granges. The direction is more or less north, and usually it is possible to see some signs of the path or previous tracks. Be careful not to descend to the east but to keep going until you come to houses. Around the back of the houses the path goes over a stream (bridge) and leads out onto a track. Ascend this to reach the rest of the buildings of Les Granges and the track towards Loriaz (see Walk 26) or descend to the village of Le Couteray and down to the main Vallorcine road. Turn right, and Le Buet is just two minutes away.

26: Refuge de Loriaz, 2020m, and Charmoz, 2366m

The alpage of Loriaz is typical, situated as it is above the tree-line, and therefore enjoying wonderful views. The alpage is owned by the commune of Vallorcine, and cattle are still taken up there for grazing in the summer. The farm buildings have been renovated into a refuge and associated buildings, maintaining the traditional rural structures. The refuge is only open in the summer

Starting point	Le Couteray
Starting altitude	1330m
Summit altitude	2020m (Refuge de Loriaz), 2366m Charmoz
Altitude gain	690m to refuge, 1036m to summit.
Time	2h to refuge, 2h round trip hut to the summit
Grade	to refuge 1, to summit 2
Aspect	SE
Map	1:25,000 IGN Top 25 3630 OT Chamonix; 1:50,000 Didier Richard C Mont Blanc
Public transport	Train Vallorcine–Le Buet–Chamonix

Access: From Chamonix take the main road south-west to the hamlet of Le Couteray. Park in the first big car park on the second bend.

months, although there are plans for winter opening in the future.

In the winter you may find the refuge almost buried by two or three metres of snow, but it is usually possible to excavate a wall to sit on whilst picnicking. The north faces of the Argentière peaks are impressive from here, as are the other major peaks of the massif, especially the Aiguille Verte and the Aiguille du Chardonnet. To the south-west you can see all the way up the Bérard valley, and to the west the Aiguillette des Posettes dominates.

The refuge itself is a fine objective for a day, but if you have energy and time to spare then it is worth extending the walk. This can be done in various ways. You can continue on towards the Col de la Terrasse. This is a popular ski tour, and while the final slope is too steep for snowshoes, the cwm underneath is perfectly feasible as long as the avalanche risk isn't high. An alternative objective is the Tête de la Chevrette, 2197m, just above the forest track used in ascent, or the Charmoz (spelt Charmo on some maps), described below. This route is often good on snowshoes, but can sometimes be to icy, so don't carry on regardless if conditions aren't favourable – remember you have got to get back down.

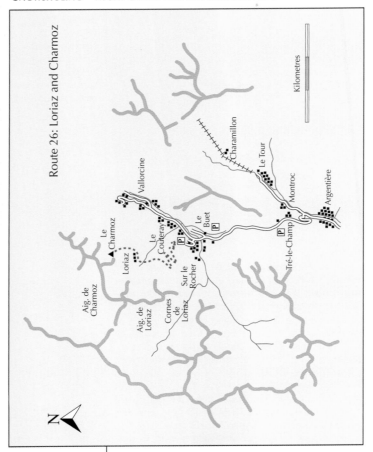

Route 26: Loriaz and Charmoz

Vallorcine

Le Charmoz

Loriaz

Le Couteray

Le Buet

Charamillon

Le Tour

Montroc

Argentière

Tré-le-Champ

Sur le Rocher

Aig. de Charmoz

Aig. de Loriaz

Cornes de Loriaz

Kilometres

N

Route

Loriaz is signed from the parking area. Take the forest track which climbs up past Les Granges; there will almost always be snowshoe and ski tracks and footprints. A little after Les Granges is an obvious junction, where the track turns left and the summer footpath continues straight ahead. There may well be tracks leading along the footpath, and this is an optional route to Loriaz. However, after recent heavy snowfall this path should be avoided as it crosses a major avalanche gully. This same gully can even cause problems during stable conditions, as the path becomes very steep and

The alpage of La Poya in Vallorcine

exposed with hard snow underfoot. Traversing this can be extremely dangerous on snowshoes, so if you choose to try this way be prepared to turn back if conditions are not easy – before you get committed mid-traverse. Do not try to descend by this route unless you have already checked it out on the ascent.

Back on the original route, the forest track continues to climb in long gentle zigzags. South-facing, this track can get pretty hot in sunny weather. Avalanche barriers above protect the way, although if the avalanche risk is high there is always the possibility of wet snow slides onto the track.

At around 2000m you emerge from the trees at a flat area, next to a tunnel entrance. The fairly steep southwest-facing slope ahead must be climbed to reach Loriaz. This can be done by traversing to the right or by going up by the pylons. It is worth making a good track here, if there isn't one already, to aid your descent. The refuge is just a few minutes away at the top of the slope.

The Charmoz is best climbed by taking a northerly line from the hut. There are rocky sections on the slope, which can be avoided by a judicious choice of line. Needless to say, in bad visibility do not go up, as it would be difficult to navigate here. Descend by the same route, taking care down the steep slope to the tunnel entrance.

27: Aiguillette des Posettes, 2201m

Access: From Argentière take the main road uphill out of town towards Switzerland. Park soon after Tré-le-Champ at a car park on the left opposite the last building on the right.

Starting point	Between Tré-le-Champ and the Col des Montets at car park
Starting altitude	1430m
Summit altitude	2201m
Altitude gain	771m + 200m to return from Vallorcine to Col des Montets
Time	6–7h round trip
Grade	2
Aspect	S, W, E, N
Map	1:25,000 IGN Top 25 3630 OT Chamonix; 1:50,000 Didier Richard C Mont Blanc
Public transport	Train Chamonix–Montroc–Vallorcine

The Aiguillette des Posettes occupies a privileged position at the head of the Chamonix valley, giving a superb vantage point for the surrounding glaciated peaks. It has been partially invaded by ski lifts and pistes, but the summit so far remains untouched, and its south-western ridge is a fine way to climb this mountain.

From the top you'll be rewarded with breathtaking views of the Chamonix valley, with the Mont Blanc massif on one side and the Aiguilles Rouges on the other, with Mont Buet standing proud. The Emosson dam is seen clearly, marking the Franco-Swiss frontier to the north. This is a place to linger and enjoy before descending to the ski area of Le Tour-Vallorcine. The easiest way down from the summit is via the Col des Posettes, Les Esserts, then the forest track which serves as a ski piste all the way back to Vallorcine. It is long and is used by skiers, but it is beautiful in the forest – follow the signs for the green piste and keep off the groomed track.

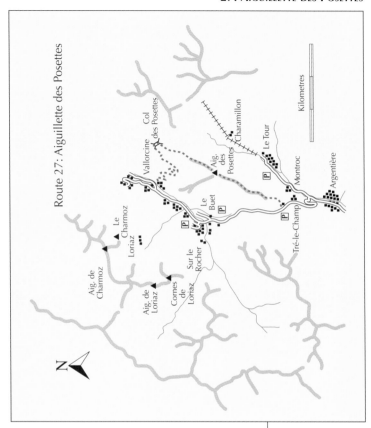

Route 27: Aiguillette des Posettes

Alternatively you could brave the faster pistes on the south side and take the lift down from the middle station at Charamillon.

The south slopes of the Aiguillette des Posettes do avalanche, especially in warm conditions. Equally, early in the morning these slopes could be icy and hard underfoot. Be prepared to meet all sorts of conditions, and do not venture here immediately after fresh snowfall.

Route

From the car park head east into the forest. You'll be able to make out traces of the summer track that is signed here to the Aiguillette des Posettes. It basically takes a northerly route uphill through the woods until it is possible to break out onto the south-west ridge of the mountain, which is followed to the top. This ridge is rocky in places, and you will probably be forced onto the south face from time to time and will have to scramble easily up the final few metres. Don't be tempted onto the north face as this is steep, and the snow may be less stable on these shady slopes. When you arrive at the summit don't be surprised to meet skiers and snowboarders launching themselves down the gullies that descend to Vallorcine – this way is not for those on snowshoes!

You can retrace you steps if you are sure that conditions are safe and that the slopes you came up have not now become dangerously hot. If you choose to descend to Vallorcine you need to go down to the Col des Posettes. Either take the ridge onwards, going north-east, or, just past the summit, drop off onto the south slopes and traverse across to the ski piste coming down from the ski lift under the summit. Then descend next to the pistes to reach the broad open col. Here signs indicate the green forest piste that takes you gently and pleasantly down to Vallorcine (as with all ski pistes, keep well to the side). This is long but the terrain is easy. To descend on the lift to Le Tour, which is not really recommended, once again go down to the Col des Posettes then follow the probably busy ski piste (taking your life in your hands!) southwards, all the way down and around to Charamillon, from where you can take the gondola lift to Le Tour.

28: Tête de Balme, 2321m

Starting point	Top of the Le Tour lift system
Starting altitude	2200m
Summit altitude	2321m
Altitude gain	130m
Time	1h30–2h
Grade	1
Aspect	SE
Map	1:25,000 IGN Top 25 3630 OT; 1:50,000 Didier Richard C Mont Blanc
Public transport	Bus Chamonix–Argentière–Le Tour

Access: From Chamonix take the main N205 road past Argentière towards Switzerland. Just after Argentière turn right to Montroc and Le Tour. Park in the big car park at the end of the road. Take the gondola lift followed by the main Col de Balme chairlift.

The Tête de Balme is on the Franco-Swiss border, just above the Col de Balme, well known to walkers of the Tour du Mont Blanc. Before the extension of the Le Tour ski area in the 1990s this small summit was popular with ski tourers and snowshoers alike for its views, relative accessibility and amenable terrain. Now it is very close to the ski lifts, but is still worthwhile as a short walk or when high avalanche risk rules out most other options above the tree-line.

The beauty of Mont Blanc is seen to great effect from the Le Tour resort, as is the uninterrupted view of the Chamonix valley. Add to that the fun of doing a peak where you can stand in two countries at once and you have a good reason to go to the Tête de Balme. However, those with a low tolerance for skiers had better abstain!

Route
From the top of the lift follow the pisted track horizontally to the Col de Balme, 2191m. The Tête de Balme is directly ahead to the north-north-west and can be ascended by more or less steep tracks depending on the

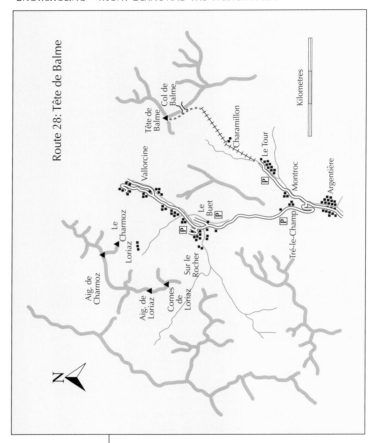

Route 28: Tête de Balme

state of your legs and the number of zigzags you do.

It is advisable to descend by the same slope, as any other way involves becoming embroiled with the skiers. Have a drink at the col café on the way back. In times past this col was the main route between the Chamonix valley and the Valais region of Switzerland, and was much travelled by traders and travellers.

SWITZERLAND
Martigny Region

Martigny

Martigny is a Roman town with a renovated amphitheatre and a castle from a later date. It also has the renowned Fondation Giannada art exhibition centre. It is placed centrally for many of the walks in the area and would make a good place to stay if you like a town atmosphere and do not mind driving each day.

Champex

Champex is to be found above the Val d'Entremont and the town of Orsières. It is a chic resort with its own lake and fantastic views of the Grand Combin. The skiing is relatively limited here and the town does not get too busy. There are all the services you need except a pharmacy.

Bourg St Pierre

Heading up towards the Grand St Bernard, this small village is the last before the pass. Famous for having lodged Napoleon I and some 40,000 troops en route to Italy, the village offers a couple of hotels and minimum but adequate facilities. It is just off the main road, which makes it very convenient.

Col de la Forclaz

Just one hotel here and a small shop, but in a prime position. It's right on the main road, near the Franco-Swiss frontier, which makes it easy to access the Martigny walks and the nearby Chamonix area walks.

Finhaut

In Victorian times Finhaut was one of the 'must-visit' places on the well-heeled traveller's list. It has lost this status to the nearby resorts, but maintains its sense of grandeur with several large hotels. It is a quiet, family-based village, sunny and well positioned for several walks as well as the train line Chamonix–Martigny. A couple of shops and a post office complete its services.

Photo: Jon de Montjoie

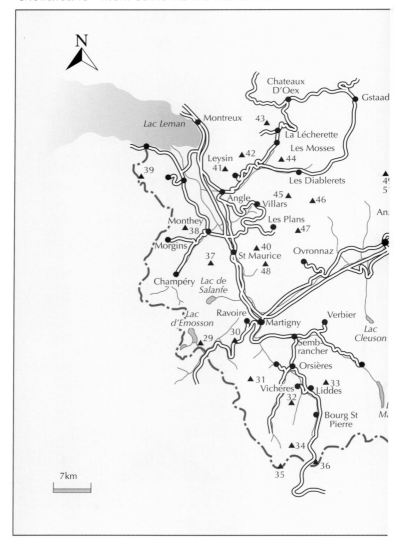

Routes 29–57: Switzerland

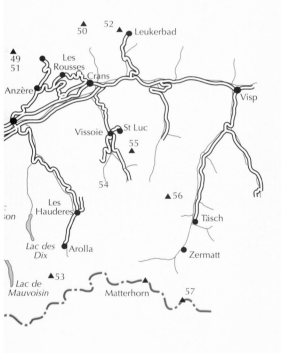

29: Emosson Lake, 1931m, Six Jeur, 2062m, and Col de la Terrasse, 2648m

Access: From Martigny take the road over the Col de la Forclaz and head towards the French border at Châtelard. Just before this, look out for a road on the right to Finhaut. Take this and go up past the village following signs to Emosson. Park where the road is closed. Finhaut is also on the train route from Martigny to Chamonix, so this walk could be done without a car.

Starting point	Finhaut
Starting altitude	1360m
Summit altitude	Emosson lake 1930m, Six Jeur 2062m, Col de la Terrasse 2648m
Altitude gain	570m to Emosson lake, additional 132m to Six Jeur, additional 720m to Col de la Terrasse
Time	2h30 to Emosson lake, 1h round trip from the lake to Six Jeur, 5h round trip lake to Col de la Terrasse
Grade	Emosson lake 1, Six Jeur 2, Col de la Terrasse 4
Aspect	S, SE, N
Map	1:25,000 Carte Nationale de la Suisse 1324 Barberine; 1:50,000 Carte Nationale de la Suisse 5003 Mont Blanc Grand Combin
Public transport	Train Martigny–Finhaut–Chamonix

Prior to 1920, high above the Vallorcine valley, the Barberine alpage was an area of alpine pastures and summer farms, perched opposite one of the most magnificent panoramas in the Alps. Then the Barberine dam was built, flooding well over half of the meadows. After this the higher Vieux Emosson lake was dammed in 1950, and finally the huge dam that we see today at Emosson was finished in 1975 after seven years of work. This feeds the hydro-electric station at Le Châtelard, which provides electricity in a joint Franco-Swiss operation.

It seems strange in a book of this kind to wax lyrical about a huge concrete man-made structure, but the Emosson dam really is rather fine. It is a pleasing curved wall, 180m high, holding back some millions of litres of

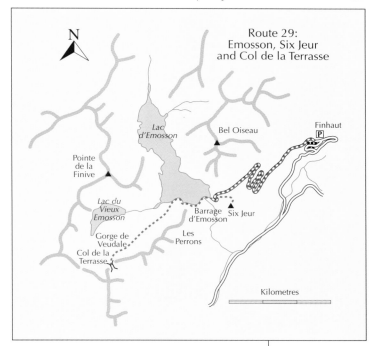

Route 29:
Emosson, Six Jeur
and Col de la Terrasse

water. It towers over the tiny hamlet of Barberine far below, creating one of the most picturesque reservoirs in the region. In winter the whole lake freezes over and breaks away from the sides, forming impressive crevasses. Many summits walks and tours exist around the dam area, but since the dam is not accessible by car in winter these tend to be quite long and arduous, and the lake itself is a good objective for a walk on snowshoes. The walk is quite long, but presents no technical difficulties. Although the ascent and descent are by the same route (the summer road) shortcuts are possible on the descent for variety and fun.

From the lake the Mont Blanc massif is seen like the backdrop to a film – from end to end with no obstructions.

Just reaching the summit of Six Jeur

The splendour of the region makes this a memorable outing – not only for the views but also on account of the special feeling of this area. In some strange way there is a wildness that rather defies the huge man-made structure, hemmed in as it is with the backdrop to the north of the Tour Sallière and the Mont Ruan, the towering Aiguille du Van to the south-west, and the rugged slopes of the Bel Oiseau just above.

The small summit of Six Jeur, just above the chapel at the Col de la Geulaz, is an good objective if you still have energy and time when you reach the lake. It is much more interesting than it looks and provides an even better view, if this is possible. The route to the top takes a rising line which manages to avoid all steep ground, taking you out onto a broad shoulder and up to the top.

A much more serious objective is the Col de la Terrasse, an arduous and quite technical expedition which should not be underestimated. The Gorge de la Veudale, which is taken to reach the col, has a secretive feel, and just venturing in there is an adventure. However, sometimes it is not possible to reach the Gorge de la Veudale on snowshoes because of steep avalanche cones, and in this case it is necessary either to go on crampons or to turn back. Lack of time may also dictate a change of plan on this walk, as it is very long. Nevertheless, on the right day in the right conditions it can be fantastic. The col is on the Franco-Swiss frontier and commands a fabulous vista of the north faces of the

Argentière summits – the Aiguille, Verte, the Droites, the Courtes and the Triolet, as well, of course, as Mont Blanc.

Route

Follow the snow-covered road all the way to the lake. The slopes above the road often avalanche immediately after fresh snowfall, so choose your day. There are places where you can take the summer path shortcuts, but these can be saved for the descent to allow a gentle climb up. At the lake cross the dam – this can be a little alarming if there is a build-up of snow as it is a big drop on both sides, especially on the left.

If you are heading for the Six Jeur, having visited the dam, go back up to the chapel at La Geulaz. The peak is climbed by following the line of summer track which winds around the north side of the summit to find a gentle route right to the top. It is worth going along to the cross.

To reach the Col de la Terrasse from the far side of the dam head around the lake, taking great care if the track is banked out by snow. There are sections to get round the Tête du Large that sometimes are too dangerous to cross on snowshoes. If in doubt turn back, as the consequences of a slip are serious. (It may be possible to take an easier line by descending to the lake and going along the flatter terrain there before climbing back up a small couloir before the inlet that receives the outflow (Nant de Drance) from the Vieux Emosson lake.) You will find the valley of the Gorge de la Veudale on the left. This valley begins with pleasant gentle slopes, but at the top it gets steeper and in some conditions may be too steep for snowshoes. If it is icy and hard it may be advisable to turn around here – remember you have to come back down the same way.

The gorge brings you out above the Vieux Emosson lake. It would be extremely easy to get lost here in bad visibility – or at night. Turn around here if you are not making good time at this point.

The route continues south in undulating terrain taking

the easiest line, as there are few natural features here. However, electricity cables provide a useful landmark, and the Col de la Terrasse is just before the big pylon. Don't let this put you off – the views are so fine that you'll soon forget about these scars on the landscape. Descend by the same route.

30: Mont de l'Arpille, 2085m

Starting point	Chez Pillet
Starting altitude	1320m
Summit altitude	2085m
Altitude gain	765m
Time	4–5h round trip
Grade	2
Aspect	N, E
Map	1:25,000 Carte Nationale de la Suisse 1325 Sembrancher 1324 Barberine; 1:50,000 Carte Nationale de la Suisse 5003 Mont Blanc Grand Combin
Public transport	Bus Martigny–Ravoire, but not up to Chez Pillet

Access: From Martigny the road climbs up towards the Col de la Forclaz. Well before this the village of Ravoire is reached by taking a turning to the right some way after the first hairpin. At the entrance to the village, follow signs to the hamlet of Chez Pillet. This is a permanently inhabited hamlet and parking is limited. If there are no places, park further down and walk up the road to this point, or take one of the signed paths that head up the hill from further down the road. They all lead to Arpille.

Perched high above the Rhône valley, the Mont de l'Arpille is a classic snowshoe summit. Beginning in a typically charming Swiss hamlet perfectly situated on a sunny hillside perch, the walk gently wanders up through larch and spruce forest to the Arpille alpage. This in itself has often proved too attractive to leave, and many people content themselves with a couple of hours sunbathing here. The Grand Combin is seen in all its splendour, whilst in the foreground is the large summit of the Pointe Ronde. However, to get the full panorama you must continue. The summit requires an hour or so more effort, but this is more than compensated by the spectacular panorama. Below is the flat-bottomed Rhône valley

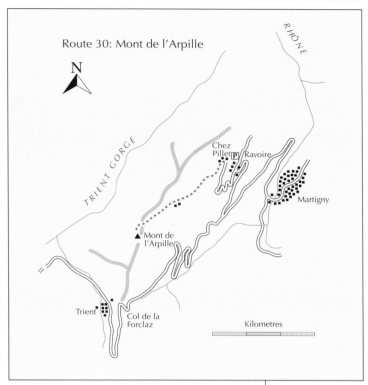

Route 30: Mont de l'Arpille

N

and the Roman town of Martigny, whilst as far as the eye can see are snowy peaks and snaking glaciers, including Mont Blanc, Mont Buet, the Bernese Oberland, the Jura and the impressive rocky west face of the Dent du Morcles.

Route

From Chez Pillet take the narrow path up into the trees behind the houses to a clearing with a couple of chalets. Behind here Arpille is signposted. The chalets of Les Clous are soon passed on the right, and it is possible

Far below the Mont de l'Arpille the Rhône valley descends from the Bernese Oberland

either to go up to these then follow the path through the forest or to stay on the forest track until a footpath is signed off to the right. You may feel a little confused in the forest as there are several forest tracks, not all of which are marked on the map, but all paths in a general south-west direction lead up through the forest to emerge at the beautiful alpage of Arpille.

From the alpage chalets carry on in the same direction up towards another forested area. Here be careful not to traverse across the steep east slopes of the peak, as these can be avalanche prone. It is better to head up steeply onto the rounded ridge then go south towards the top. The final stage is magical, winding in and out of the trees, through rolling slopes, to finish on the flat summit.

It is possible to descend directly to the Col de la Forclaz by taking the western slopes of the peak and then going steeply down through the forest to the south (you would need to have left a car here or to take the bus back down to Martigny). Alternatively, return by the same route to Chez Pillet, which is my preference, if only for the joy of running down the perfectly angled slopes above the alpage.

31: Arpette Valley, 2000m, and Col des Ecandies, 2796m

Starting point	La Breya chairlift car park
Starting altitude	1498m
Summit altitude	Relais d'Arpette 1660m, Col des Ecandies 2796m
Altitude gain	102m to Relais, 1298m to col
Time	1–2h Relais round trip, 7h col round trip
Grade	Relais 1, col 2/3
Aspect	NE
Map	1:25,000 Carte Nationale de la Suisse 1345 Orsières; 1:50,000 Carte Nationale de la Suisse 5003 Mont Blanc Grand Combin
Public transport	Bus Martigny–Orsières–Champex

Access: From Martigny drive up to Sembrancher then onwards to Orsières and up to Champex. Go through the village to the La Breya chairlift car park, on the left after an obvious bend in the road.

The Arpette valley is situated above the attractive village of Champex and provides easy walking in a beautiful area. The Col des Ecandies is a harder proposition, but worth it in the right conditions. When you enter the valley you are greeted by the rugged, spiky skyline formed by the Aiguille d'Orny, Pointe d'Orny and the Pointe des Ecandies. Whether you decide to go on all the way to the Col des Ecandies or not, a circuit can be made above the Relais d'Arpette before returning via this café for a drink and time to savour the surroundings. You should however only venture into the valley above the Relais d'Arpette when the snow conditions are stable – the steep slopes which form this valley are often the scene of large avalanches after fresh snow.

The Col des Ecandies provides a magnificent belvedere from which to gaze at the Trient Glacier, in one direction beginning its chaotic tumble down to

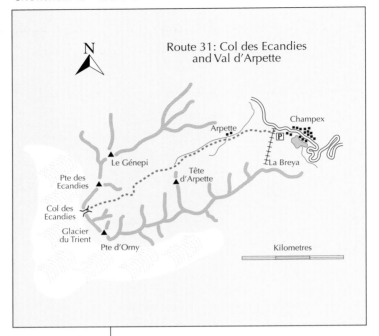

Route 31: Col des Ecandies
and Val d'Arpette

N

Champex

Arpette

P

La Breya

Le Génepi

Tête
d'Arpette

Pte des
Ecandies

Col des
Ecandies

Glacier
du Trient

Pte d'Orny

Kilometres

the valley, in the other a beautiful plateau, with the bastion of the Aiguille du Tour at its source.

The Arpette valley serves as a descent for ski tourers embarked on the Chamonix Zermatt Haute Route, so expect to see a few sweaty souls laden with rucksacks whooshing down the slopes.

Route

Do not take the La Breya chairlift (it doesn't go where you want to), but rather walk up the track in the forest. This is also used by cross-country skiers so keep well off the piste. After about 30 minutes the route reaches the Relais d'Arpette. From here follow the valley north-east. The Col des Ecandies is obvious at the head of the valley, flanked by steep pinnacles and buttresses. You can go all

Mountains and clouds vie for position

the way or just as far as seems reasonable, but be aware of the steepening walls as you get deeper into the valley. The buttress of the Tête d'Arpette cuts into the valley from the left at around 2000m, and if you are just planning a short day out this is a good place to turn around. Otherwise continue in the same direction. The north-facing slopes on the left are steep and long, and avalanches from these slopes often come all the way down to the valley. However, as the south-facing slopes to the right get steeper you are forced towards these northern slopes. As you approach to the col the terrain becomes considerably steeper, but there is nothing technical to be surmounted.

Descend by the same route. From the flat area after the Tête d'Arpette you can make a circuit by returning further to the right as you descend, making your way through the sparse forest to emerge onto the main track near the restaurant.

32: Tour de Bavon, 2476m, and Bec Rond, 2563m

Access: From
Martigny take the
road towards the
Grand St Bernard
pass and tunnel. Turn
off the main road at
Liddes, direction
Dranse, then con-
tinue up to Vichères
and beyond to Petit
Vichères, the parking
area for the ski lifts.
Take the chairlift.

Starting point	Top of the Petit Vichères chairlift
Starting altitude	2043m
Summit altitude	Tour de Bavon 2476m, Bec Rond 2563m
Altitude gain	Tour de Bavon 433m, Bec Rond 520m
Time	5–6h round trip; less if descent is on chairlift
Grade	Tour de Bavon 3, Bec Rond 2/3
Aspect	N, W, S
Map	1:25,000 Carte Nationale de la Suisse 1345 Orsières; 1:50,000 Carte Nationale de la Suisse 5003 Mont Blanc Grand Combin

You could walk this route without undertaking either of
the summits and still enjoy a great day out with breathtaking views. The Bec Rond and the Tour de Bavon are
accessed from a chairlift in the little-known ski resort of
Vichères. The word 'belvedere' must have been invented
for this place, as it occupies a privileged position within

*Returning after an
ascent of the Tour de
Bavon, seen behind
on the left*

164

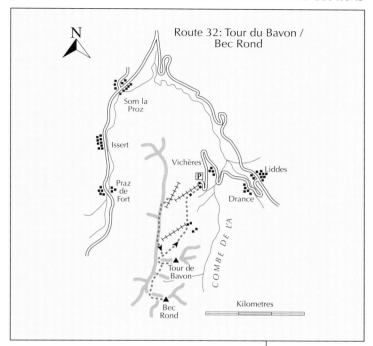

Route 32: Tour du Bavon /
Bec Rond

sight of the French and Italian borders. It is therefore sur-
rounded by many of the big names of the region – the
Mont Dolent, Aiguille d'Argentière, Mont Velan and the
Grand Combin, to name just a few.

It is difficult to decide which of the two possible
summits to climb, since both are very accessible. The
Tour de Bavon is the nearer option, but it is not much further to the Bec Rond. Both have some steep ground and
should be avoided not only in unstable conditions but
also if you are not happy to ascend and descend steep
slopes on foot. The walk from the top of the chairlift to
the flat area of Entre les Deux Tours, and then on towards
the Bec Rond, is worthwhile in itself, and the summits are
just the icing on the cake if all conditions are right

Route

From the top of the chairlift make your way up rightwards towards the rounded ridge which runs up from the Plan de la Vuardette across the track of a drag-lift. Keep to the far side of the pistes and enjoy the great views of the east faces of the Argentière peaks. Keep to the crest, above impressively steep slopes down to the Ferret valley, and pass the top of the ski pistes. In the same line head south to the slight col at La Tèjere. The impressive north face of the Tour de Bavon is clearly visible from here, but luckily the as yet hidden south face is rather more amenable.

Steeper slopes soon lead up past a memorial cairn, a salutary reminder that even small slopes like this can be deadly in the wrong conditions. A few zigzags take you onto the flat plateau of Entre les Deux Tours, where it's decision time. Turn left for the **Tour de Bavon**, winding up through interesting rock formations to the base of the south face. This is a favourite place for chamois, and you will doubtless see signs of them. It is also a good place to stop if you don't like steep slopes. However, all snow-shoes will be left here, as the final southern slope must be ascended on foot without snowshoes. This slope should be treated with caution, especially when icy, since a slip high up would be serious. Once the steep slope is ascended, a final teeter along the ridge leads to the summit. Views are splendid – a full 360° panorama as befits a true summit, with just room to sit down whilst peering over the steep north slopes. Be very careful, as the north face is even steeper than the south, and it would be easy to overbalance here. There is always a cornice, so don't go too near the edge. Descend by the same slope, facing into the slope if necessary.

For the **Bec Rond** go across the easy flat terrain of Entre les Deux Tours to a steepening, where the route joins a slope that runs all the way down into the Combe de l'A. This is climbed by judicious zigzags before reaching a delicate rocky section at around 2544m which takes you to the top. In unstable snow conditions the long snow slope can be very dangerous and should not be crossed. In such conditions the subsidiary summit,

The impressive summit of the Tour de Bavon

Further Options

From the summit of the Bec Rond it is possible to descend to the Combe de l'A. This should only be undertaken in good snow conditions when the avalanche risk is limited. The descent is via La Sasse, then down a couloir near La Tsissette to arrive at spot height 1952m in the valley.

marked as spot height 2390, provides a good objective and gives precipitous views down to the valley below. Return from the summit by the same route and back across Entre les Deux Tours.

For both routes, it is perfectly reasonable to use the chairlift on the descent, in which case be sure to buy a return ticket and not to miss the last lift down. Otherwise, leave the ascent route at the base of the steep slope with the cairn and head north-east down the pleasant valley, where you will probably find fabulous deep snow, to the buildings at Bavon. Then make your way north across the ski area, keeping off the pistes as much as possible, until under the chairlift, then slip, slide and flounder down as best you can through the trees to the restaurant at the bottom.

33: Mont Rogneux, 3084m

The summit of Mont Rogneux (photo: JP Ferlin)

Starting point	Junction beyond Lourtier on the Fionnay road
Starting altitude	1302m
Summit altitude	Cabane Brunet 2103m, summit 3084m
Altitude gain	801m to hut, 981m to the summit
Time	3h to hut, 6h round trip from the hut
Grade	3
Aspect	NE
Map	1:25,000 Carte Nationale de la Suisse 1236 Rosablanche, 1346 Chanrion, 1345 Orsières; 1:50,000 Carte Nationale de la Suisse 5003 Mont Blanc Grand Combin
Public transport	Bus Martigny–Sembrancher–Champsec–Lourtier–Fionnay. Ask to get off at pt 1302.
Accommodation	Cabane Brunet. This is a private hut, and reservations are essential. Tel: 027 778 1810, 079 628 4916

Access: From Martigny drive up to Sembrancher then past Le Châble and onwards to Champsec and then Lourtier. Continue beyond the village on the road which crosses the river and heads up towards Fionnay. After several hairpin bends there is a junction where the road goes left to Fionnay. Park here. (Both early and late in the season you can drive up the right-hand branch as far as 1600m on a rough track.)
NB There is another Mont Rogneux, just east of Verbier; the one described in this route is south of the Val de Bagnes.

Mont Rogneux is a big summit, a major undertaking on snowshoes requiring two days (with an overnight at the Cabane Brunet) and a good level of fitness. It is a summit to aspire to, and to save for the end of a season or holiday when you've got plenty of other walks under your belt. It requires stable conditions, so should be envisaged in early spring.

The north side of the Val de Bagnes has been heavily developed for skiing, but the south side remains largely untouched. Mont Rogneux forms the northern extremity of the massif that ultimately culminates in the Grand Combin. Whilst flanked on one side by imposing glaciated peaks, to the north Mont Rogneux enjoys uninterrupted views over to the Rhône valley and beyond, whilst to the west the panorama is completed by the snowy giants of the Mont Blanc massif.

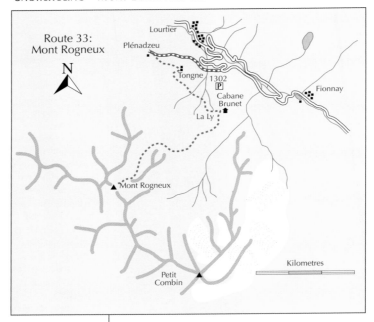

Route 33:
Mont Rogneux

N

Lourtier
Plénadzeu
Tongne
1302
P
Cabane
Brunet
La Ly
Fionnay
Mont Rogneux
Petit
Combin
Kilometres

Take the time to explore the Val de Bagnes en route, famous among other things for its cheese, which is used in the local speciality of *raclette*.

Route
Head up the track to Plénadzeu. From here, either follow the snowed-up road which climbs gently to reach the open slopes of La Ly or attain this point more rapidly by traversing south-east from Pléndzeu to the buildings of Tongne and then up through the forest.

The hut, Cabane Brunet, perched on a small promontory overlooking the Val de Bagnes, its aerial visible from afar, is easily reached by heading left (south-east) from La Ly. From the hut take gently angled slopes south-west until the plateau of Goli des Otanes. Pass to the right of the rocky buttress at pt 2776, and then head up to join the rounded east ridge of Mont Rogneux at about the point where the ridge swings round to the north-east. This is followed to the summit, at first staying on its right flank, then following the ridge proper.

Descend by the same route.

34: Col du Bastillon, 2757m, and Monts Telliers, 2851m

Starting point	Super St Bernard car park
Starting altitude	1927m
Summit altitude	Col du Bastillon 2757m, Monts Telliers 2851m
Altitude gain	830m to Col du Bastillon, 924m to Monts Telliers
Time	5h round trip to col, 6–7h round trip to summit
Grade	To the col 2, to the summit 2/3
Aspect	E, SE
Map	1:25,000 Carte Nationale de la Suisse 1365 Grand St Bernard; 1:50,000 Carte Nationale de la Suisse 5003 Mont Blanc Grand Combin
Public transport	Bus Orsières–Bourg St Bernard

Access: From Martigny drive up towards the Grand St Bernard Tunnel. Just before the customs post and tunnel payment office, leave the tunnel by an exit on the right which is quite easy to miss. Park at the large ski lift car park at Super St Bernard.

The highest of the Monts Telliers forms the high point on the long ridge that runs north to south above the Swiss Val Ferret. Any point along this ridge gives superb views of the Mont Blanc massif, but the Col du Bastillon and Mont Telliers are perhaps the best of all. From here the Grandes Jorasses are seen in profile, presenting a steep and impressive north face, whilst behind are the spectacular rocky buttresses of the Italian side of Mont Blanc, capped by its snowy summit dome.

The walk to the Monts Telliers is long, and the final section can be steep and awkward on snowshoes,

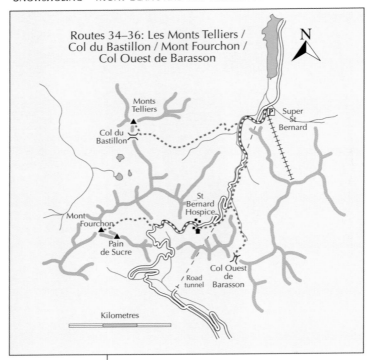

Routes 34–36: Les Monts Telliers /
Col du Bastillon / Mont Fourchon /
Col Ouest de Barasson

depending on the snow conditions. The route to the Col du Bastillon is therefore also suggested, being easier to reach, close to the summits and giving just as good a view.

The terrain around here provides ample opportunity to lose your bearings in bad weather, so be sure to look at the map and use terrain features, such as the Drône valley, in the event of poor visibility.

Route

Take the very obvious snowed-up road from the car park which goes up to the Grand St Bernard Col and Hospice. *Randonneurs* are advised to stay to the right,

and it is wise to heed this advice, as this is a ski piste and skiers will be descending fast. After about 500m take a turn off to the right, over the river and into the Combe de Drône. Initial steep slopes soon ease and the terrain becomes very pleasant and rolling. You can either remain in the valley and follow this to its end or take the slopes up on the right past Godegotte to the Grand Lé lake (which will be covered in snow, so not very obvious). If you have followed the bed of the valley head up to the Grand Lé. From here the Col de Bastillon is reached by taking a rising line to the west. For the Monts Telliers there are two options as you reach the steep slopes behind Grand Lé. Either head slightly north then directly west, or go west above the rocks to the north of the Col du Bastillon and make your way onto the south ridge of the Monts Telliers to the summit. It is a question of finding the easiest way according to the snow conditions. Descend by the same route.

From Monts Telliers the north face of the Grandes Jorasses is impressively steep and foreboding

35: Mont Fourchon, 2902m

Access: From
Martigny take the
road towards the
Grand St Bernard
pass and tunnel.
Once in the tunnel,
just before the cus-
toms post, there is an
exit on the right.
Don't miss this or
you'll end up in Italy.
Park in the ski area
(Super St Bernard)
car park.

Starting point	Super St Bernard car park
Starting altitude	1927m
Summit altitude	2902m
Altitude gain	542m to the hospice, 550m to the summit of Mont Fourchon
Time	2h each way to the hospice, 4h–4h30 hospice to summit round trip
Grade	2
Aspect	E
Map	1:25,000 Carte Nationale de la Suisse 1365 Gd St Bernard; 1:50,000 Carte Nationale de la Suisse 5003 Mont Blanc Grand Combin
Accommodation	Hospice du Grand St Bernard, which is open all year. Tel: 027 787 1236
Public transport	Bus Martigny–Orsières–Super St Bernard

The Grand St Bernard pass links Switzerland to Italy and has long been used by travellers. In the past, like all such routes, this pass was a dangerous place for travellers, who not only risked the vagaries of the weather but also attack by highwaymen. Since the 11th century there has been some sort of shelter for travellers at the col, the first hospice being set up by St Bernard, who later became the patron saint of alpinists. The Grand St Bernard Hospice is now not only a monastery with an impressive chapel and crypt, but it also offers accommodation and has a fascinating museum. In winter the road over the St Bernard pass is closed and access to the hospice is on foot – on snowshoes or skis. For those undertaking any of the summits in this area, an overnight stay at the hospice is recommended, in itself a very interesting and special experience. Mont Fourchon, 2902m, is a classic snow-shoe peak, and the views of the Mont Blanc massif are superlative. It is also possible to combine this with an ascent of the neighbouring Pain de Sucre, 2900m. This latter looks like a miniature Matterhorn when viewed from the hospice, but is in fact very accessible.

Route

From the car park take the obvious snowed-up continuation of the road around the hillside. Signs warn that this is a ski piste and that *randonneurs* should stay to the right – ignore this warning at your peril!

Some way along the track a piste comes in from the left – this is the source of most of the skiers, although some will also be descending from the hospice. Stay on the road and continue heading south into the sinister-sounding Combe des Morts. There is a basic shelter here that can provide precious respite in cold and windy conditions. Instead of following the road here it is usual to

Monks setting off on skis from the Grand St Bernard Hospice

175

take a straight line up the base of the valley. However, be aware that there are steep slopes above on both sides, and in the event of an avalanche any walker here would be a sitting duck.

The Col du Grand St Bernard is at the head of the cwm and the hospice is visible as you approach. The entrance to the hospice is on the left under the covered way.

From the hospice go around or across the ice- and snow-covered lake to rejoin the road at the frontier post. Follow the road around the hillside and through the snowed-up road tunnel which leads to the buildings of Montagna Baus. Head up west towards Mont Fourchon, keeping to the north of the Tours des Fous, under the south slopes of the Fenêtre de Ferret. The angle steepens somewhat as you get higher, and at about 2700m a long traverse should be made left, swinging back right just below the summit, where snowshoes are removed to climb the final few metres on foot. A thrilling panorama awaits you, and will probably keep you there for some time.

Most people descend from here on the same route back to the hospice. However, if you have the time and energy, and if conditions permit, the Pain de Sucre is within easy reach. Descend from the summit, and on snowshoes cross undulating ground south-eastwards to the deep col between Mont Fourchon and the Pain de Sucre. This col is hidden from view when you're on the summit of Mont Fourchon. Leaving snowshoes here, follow the steep slope (if the slope is icy, you would be advised to leave this peak for another day) then the ridge to the summit. Return by the same route to your snowshoes. From here you can retrace your steps to rejoin the ascent track or descend directly to join it lower down and follow it back via the hospice to the car park. This peak is only possible in suitable conditions, and if in doubt best not to attempt it – Mont Fourchon is a very satisfying achievement in its own right.

Further Options The Tête de Fonteinte via the Fenêtre d'en Haut makes for an easier outing that can be envisaged in the same day as you go up to the hospice. Approach is as for the Mont Fourchon, then take obvious slopes up to the north of Montagna Baus.

36: Col Ouest de Barasson, 2635m

Starting point	Super St Bernard car park
Starting altitude	1927m
Summit altitude	2635m
Altitude gain	708m
Time	4h30 round trip, or about the same if you go on up to the hospice
Grade	2
Aspect	N
Map	1:25,000 Carte Nationale de la Suisse 1365 Gd St Bernard; 1:50,000 Carte Nationale de la Suisse 5003 Mont Blanc Grand Combin
Accommodation	Hospice du Grand St Bernard, which is open all winter. Tel: 027 787 1236
Public transport	Bus Martigny–Orsières–Super St Bernard

Access: From Martigny take the road towards the Grand St Bernard pass and tunnel. Once in the tunnel, just before the customs post, there is an exit on the right. Don't miss this or you'll end up in Italy. Park in the ski area (Super St Bernard) car park.

This is an option to do on the way up to the Grand St Bernard Hospice. Although this hillside is rather spoiled by the high-tension electricity lines, this col is nevertheless a good walk, both for the views and the fact that it makes a day of the ascent to the hospice. Once under the cables just before the col you are hardly aware of them, as your gaze is held by the magnificence of the vista appearing before your eyes – Mont Blanc, the formidable north face on the Grandes Jorasses seen in profile, and all the surrounding splendour of snowy peaks and dark valleys. The Barasson cwm in the past saw considerable passage from smugglers taking goods such as tobacco over the border from Switzerland into Italy.

A good descent from the Col Ouest de Barasson

Further Options The Col Est de Barasson is also possible, but the final slope is steep and is usually done on foot. It can also present a risk of avalanche in certain snow conditions.

Route

From the car park head up the snowed-up Col du Grand St Bernard road until you can see the second bandstand-type building, which is in fact a ventilation shaft for the tunnel, at Les Tronchets, 2276m. Before reaching this you can head left into the Combe de Barasson, following the electricity cables. Choose the best way up the valley towards the metal cross commemorating the death of Lucien Droz, a monk from the hospice who was killed with several others in an avalanche which came down from the slopes of Mont Mort in 1951. Just before reaching the mound on which the memorial is sited take the slope between Mont Mort and the Tête de Barasson to reach the Col Ouest de Barasson between the two. This is the Swiss-Italian frontier. Return by the same route as far as Les Tronchets, then turn left if you are going on up to the hospice.

AIGLE REGION

Aigle
Aigle is surrounded by villages which would all make great bases for a snowshoe walking holiday. Aigle itself is pleasant, not too industrialised, with easy access to both sides of the Rhône valley.

Leysin
A popular ski resort with lots of hotels and shops. Leysin is not the place to go if you want a quiet time, but will appeal to those who want somewhere lively.

Villars
Villars is quite a large town, not only catering to the skiers but also to all winter holiday-makers. It

offers typical Swiss accommodation, and there are some calm and tranquil spots. Very well placed for lots of walks in the area.

Diablerets
Another very pleasant typical Swiss village, slightly smaller than some of its neighbours.

Trois Torrents/Val d'Illiez/ Champéry
All three of these villages or small towns would provide a good base for walking, with Champéry being the most ski-orientated. They all offer the usual traditional Swiss alpine hospitality, combining charm with efficiency.

37: Dent de Valerette, 2059m

A classic snowshoe peak ideally provides interesting and varied terrain, both below and above the tree-line, and stunning views. The Dent de Valerette fits the bill perfectly. Its relatively gentle ascent route, beginning in the forest, emerges at intervals then culminates with a final climb up to the summit cross, where you are greeted with the breathtaking spectacle of the impressive north face of the Dents du Midi.

Whilst the Dent de Valerette is accessible to ski tourers from the tiny resort of Les Giettes, the pistes can be largely avoided by snowshoers, and the proximity of the resort does not detract from this fine outing. In fact the pistes here are rarely crowded even at weekends, and there is little chance of meeting lots of skiers.

Access: From Aigle go to Monthey then head up to Les Cerniers. Park as for the ski lifts.

Starting point	Les Cerniers
Starting altitude	1291m
Summit altitude	2059m
Altitude gain	768m
Time	4-5h round trip
Grade	2
Aspect	NE, N
Map	1:25,000 Carte Nationale de la Suisse 1304 Val d'Illiez; 1:50,000 Carte Nationale de la Suisse 272 Saint Maurice
Public transport	Bus Monthey–Les Cerniers

Route

From Les Cerniers take the path directly south which goes up to the forest track leading to Les Plans at 1401m. From here go south to Les Jeurs via a very pleasant clearing in the trees. At Les Jeurs there is another track, usually pisted, leading around to the ski pistes and restaurant at Chindonne. Be careful to stay well to the edge of the pistes, and make your way up to the top of the drag-lift (south-west). From here find a long clearing in the forest directly behind the small building, and follow this until it eventually emerges from the trees onto gentle slopes. Now take the rounded north ridge of the Dent de Valerette to the cross on the summit.

To descend, head a short way along the summit ridge towards the Pointe de l'Erse before going down to the farm of Valerette. Return to the shoulder at the top of the lift, from where you can follow signed paths leftwards down into the forest and onwards directly to Les Cerniers. (If the summit ridge is corniced return to the shoulder by the ascent route.)

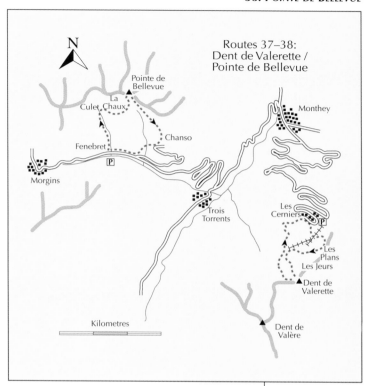

Routes 37–38:
Dent de Valerette /
Pointe de Bellevue

In exceptional snow conditions it may be possible to descend to Trois Torrents: from Valerette take the track west then descend north-east via forest and clearings by Bonevouette to Les Fahys, from where you follow the road over the river. Take the train back to Monthey.

38: Pointe de Bellevue, 2042m

Aptly named, the Pointe de Bellevue is an accessible peak which is climbed for its *belle vue* of Lac Léman, the Rhône valley and to the south the imposing north face of the Dents du Midi. The relatively modest altitude of this peak belies its lofty feel, perched as it is with nothing between it and the flat valley 1600m below.

Access: From Aigle go to Monthey, Trois Torrents, then up the main road towards Morgins. Park at Fenebet, which is about 2.5km before Morgins.

Starting point	Fenebet
Starting altitude	1260m
Summit altitude	2042m
Altitude gain	780m
Time	4h round trip
Grade	1
Aspect	S
Map	1:25,000 Carte Nationale de la Suisse 1304 Val d'Illiez, 1284 Monthey; 1:50,000 Carte Nationale de la Suisse 272 Saint Maurice
Public transport	Bus Monthey–Morgins

The gentle slopes of the Pointe de Bellevue are a perfect place to snowshoe, and you are not restricted in terms of routes – just go where the snow looks best and make your track. Don't be too surprised to meet lots of people here, especially at weekends, as it is justifiably popular and can be attacked by different routes, one of which starts from the ski lifts of Morgins.

Route
Go straight up to Les Cadraux, then follow the right bank of the stream to the flatter area of Culet. Traverse right (east) and up to the sloping plateau of La Chaux and on up to the summit of the Pointe de Bellevue.

To descend, follow the south-east arête until you can head right (west) to the chalets at Chanso. Continue the descent through clearings and forest then head across to the right, crossing a stream when you can, to come out on the road less than 1km below the car park.

Cutting a block in the snow and seeing how easily it slides is one way to assess avalanche risk

39: Lac de Tanay, 1408m, and Col d'Ugeon, 2019m

Starting point	Le Flon
Starting altitude	1050m
Summit altitude	Lac de Tanay 1408m, Col d'Ugeon 2019m
Altitude gain	358m to lake, 611m to col
Time	1h to lake, 6–7h round trip from lake
Grade	to Tanay 1, to Col d'Ugeon 2/3
Aspect	E
Map	1:25,000 Carte Nationale de la Suisse 1284 Monthey; 1:50,000 Carte Nationale de la Suisse 271 Chablais, 272 St Maurice
Public transport	Bus Aigle–Vouvry–Le Flon

Access: From Aigle drive across the Rhône to Vionnaz then Vouvry. Here turn left and up to Miex. Continue on to Le Flon and park at car park at the far side of the village.

The Col d'Ugeon is a pleasant outing on snowshoes which, although not difficult, is quite long and should not be attempted after fresh snow, as the nearby slopes are very steep and avalanche prone. Tanay lake itself is worth visiting, surrounded as it is by the steep rocky

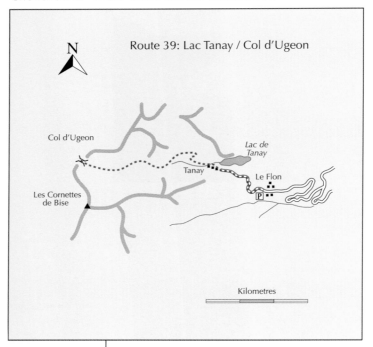

Route 39: Lac Tanay / Col d'Ugeon

N

Col d'Ugeon

Lac de Tanay

Tanay

Le Flon

P

Les Cornettes de Bise

Kilometres

summits of Les Jumelles, Alamon and Le Sechon. However, do note that even when the track up to Tanay is clear of snow, it is authorised only for four-wheel-drive vehicles.

En route to the Col d'Ugeon, if you find yourself weary by the time you reach the farm buildings of Montagne de l'Au, you would be advised to turn back, as the col is a lot further than it appears. This walk is delightful wherever you get to, as it takes you into a wild and unfrequented area, beautiful in the snow, with the impressive steep walls of the Cornettes de Bise, 2432m, the highest summit in the region, to the south. Keep your eyes open for chamois and ibex. If you arrive at the flat Col d'Ugeon, you have reached the Franco-Swiss border.

Route

From Le Flon follow the wide jeep track up through the forest. Alternatively, cut up via the footpath which may or may not be visible in the snow. The Col de Tanay cannot be missed, and here you descend slightly as you go along to the village of Tanay.

The summer path up the valley above Tanay is not recommended in winter as it is threatened by avalanches and also goes very close to the river, which will be snow-covered and consequently difficult to avoid. There is a jeep track up to the Montagne de l'Au farm that can be followed on the north side of the valley. Even here expect to encounter avalanche debris, which can be awkward to cross. The track goes through a tunnel that may be icy or blocked by snow. Finally the terrain becomes easier as you near the farm of Montagne de l'Au. Continue on over undulating ground, all the time heading west-north-west towards the Col d'Ugeon, which is the lowest point directly ahead. The varying angles make for interesting walking combined with the views of the surrounding peaks. Eventually you will find the flat col, and the frontier with France is just below on the west side. Descend by the same route, picking the best line for descent on the short steeper slopes.

40: Croix de Javerne, 2097m

The summit of the Croix de Javerne is reached by a narrow, snowy arête, the west side of which plunges straight down to the Rhône valley. Lac Léman is close by, often shrouded in mist, whilst the snow-topped Chablais peaks stand proud on the other side of the valley. To the south, guarding the head of the Javerne valley, are the rocky ramparts of the Dent de Morcles, mirroring the equally impressive summits of the Dents du Midi just to the west.

This is a summit to savour, from the beginnings of the path way down in the forest, where animal tracks bear testament to much nocturnal and early morning activity, to the gradual climb through glades and meadows up to

Access: From Aigle go to Bex then up towards Gryon, turning off to Les Plans sur Bex. Park opposite a turn off marked Javerne.

Starting point	Les Plans sur Bex
Starting altitude	1070m
Summit altitude	2097m
Altitude gain	1027m
Time	6h round trip
Grade	2
Aspect	N, E
Map	1:25,000 Carte Nationale de la Suisse 1285 Les Diablerets, 1305 Dent de Morcles; 1:50000 272 St Maurice
Public transport	Bus/tram Aigle–Bex, bus Bex–Les Plans sur Bex

the charming hamlet of Javerne, and then the increasingly steep winding ascent to the summit.

Whilst the first few steps down the ridge may give pause for thought as to the consequences of a misplaced snowshoe, you'll soon find your pace, and those who enjoy a good run down will doubtless launch off down the east slopes directly to the Javerne valley.

Route

Take the road signed to Javerne. At the first leftwards hairpin there is a track going straight on that is similarly signed to Javerne. In good snow cover this can make for a useful shortcut. Otherwise, continue on the road. If you take the track be sure not to miss the ascending path up to meet the road again. If you go along the road there is a junction after the second leftwards hairpin signed right to Les Colatels and left to Javerne. Take the right-hand road and continue along this. You'll meet the other footpath at a bridge.

The flat road continues over a ravine and then fades out just before a clearing in the trees. Continue the traverse and you'll see a chalet above. Go up to this, then take a southerly direction through the forest. Continue

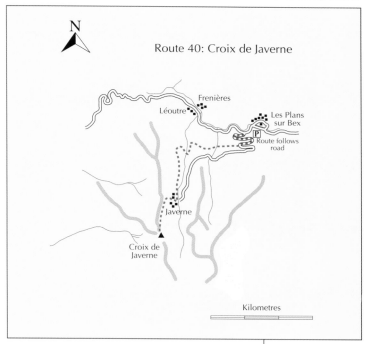

Route 40: Croix de Javerne

N

Frenières
Léoutre
Les Plans
sur Bex
P
Route follows
road

Javerne

Croix de
Javerne

Kilometres

past another chalet to finally reach the hamlet of Javerne.
The other road comes in from the left here.

The Croix de Javerne is easy to spot now on the
snow arête forming the west side of the valley. Head
straight up the slopes west of Javerne, and about 100m
higher you'll see a signpost in the trees showing the
Croix de Javerne to the left and Châtillon to the right. A
rising traverse left brings you out onto the snowy crest
just before the Tête de Niouston. The rest of the route is
unmistakable, taking the ridge right to the top.

Either descend by the same route or, if the snow is
not icy and you fancy a blast, take a right at the Tête de
Niouston and bound down to Javerne by these superb
slopes. It is possible to return by the road on the far side

Further Options
Châtillon makes for a
shorter option: from
Javerne head up west
and take the right-
hand path at the
signpost to head up
north-west to the
summit.

187

The Croix de Javerne, with the Dent de Morcles behind

of the valley from Javerne or to enjoy the rest of the descent through Les Colatels before picking up the lower road.

41: Solacyre, 1845m, and Riondaz, 1981m

Access: From Leysin town centre drive up towards Feyday along the road which finishes at Prarea. Just before this there is a quarry on the right. Park here, or as near to this as possible.

Starting point	Leysin quarry
Starting altitude	1471m
Summit altitude	1981m
Altitude gain	510m
Time	3–3h30
Grade	to Solacyre 1, to La Riondaz 2
Aspect	S
Map	1:25,000 Carte Nationale de la Suisse 1284 Monthey; 1:50,000 Carte Nationale de la Suisse 272 Saint Maurice

This is a very pleasant walk either for a first day or when weather or snow conditions preclude going higher. La Riondaz forms the high point of the ridge which runs from Aigle all the way up to Berneuse at the top of the

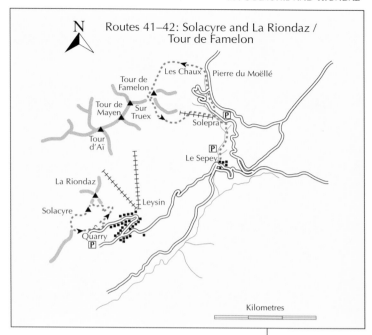

Routes 41–42: Solacyre and La Riondaz / Tour de Famelon

Leysin lift system, and gives an uninterrupted vista of the not so far off Lac Léman and the lakeside towns of Montreux and Villeneuve. Above the lake are the Chablais peaks, including the characteristic double summits of Les Jumelles. The walk takes you well away from the lifts to enjoy the forest, which is beautiful when snow covered, and the unusual views down to the Rhône valley.

Route

From the quarry head up the track by Les Lapies, quite steep at first but soon easing off in the forest towards Joux des Vents. The building of Le Temeley is visible as you emerge into a clearing, but you need to head west from here up to a col just beneath Solacyre, easily identified by a disused chairlift building. Whilst the old chairlift should soon be dismantled, the building will remain for use as a private *dortoir*. The summit of Solacyre (1845m) is just above to the south.

In bad weather this could be the objective for the day. If conditions allow, then La Riondaz is only another 30 minutes away, and is reached by the ridge directly above to the north.

Descend either by the same route or, from Solacyre, a better way is to go down the attractive rounded ridge into the forest and out to Prafandaz. Here there are superb views down to the valley. A track leads around eastwards back to the road and the quarry.

42: Tour de Famelon, 2138m

The rocky bastion of the Tour de Famelon does not at first present itself as a typical snowshoe summit, as there appears to be no reasonable route to the summit. In fact appearance is deceptive, and the peak goes perfectly well on foot and is a superb outing, both for the variety and beauty of terrain and for the spectacular views. The route to the summit also provides several other alternative snowshoe objectives along the way. The Pierre du Moëllé at the head of the valley is itself a charming spot for a picnic, and the nearby rounded tops of Les Chaux can be the aim of a moderate day, when you just want to enjoy a walk in the sun or when conditions are not suitable for the ascent of a peak. From the Pierre du Moëllé views of the Mont Blanc massif are superb. The continuation onwards towards the Tour de Famelon takes a delightfully intricate route around the other side of the summit. It emerges at a col, from where you can ascend the Tour de Famelon on foot, continue on snowshoes to Sur Truex or do neither of these possibilities, but descend from here back to the valley. The descent also presents two options – either return by the same route, varying the way according to the slopes, or take a steeper route which goes down to join the ski pistes leading down to

Starting point	Le Sepey, Solepra or Pierre du Moëllé
Starting altitude	974m at Le Sepey, 1350m at Solepra, 1661m at Pierre du Moëllé
Summit altitude	Tour de Famelon 2138m
Altitude gain	788m Tour de Famelon from Solepra. Add on 380m from Le Sepey, subtract 311 from Pierre du Moëllé.
Time	Add on 1h30 from Le Sepey. 5hs round trip Solepra–Tour de Famelon
Grade	Tour de Famelon 2/3
Aspect	S, E, N, W
Map	1:25,000 Carte Nationale de la Suisse 1265 Les Mosses; 1:50,000 Carte Nationale de la Suisse 262 Rochers de Naye
Public transport	Bus Aigle–Le Sepey

Access: From Aigle take the road towards Les Mosses, Diablerets and Leysin. At the junction up to Leysin is the small village of Le Sepey. The walk can begin here if the snow level is low enough. However, it is worth checking if the road up to Solepra or even the Pierre du Moëllé is open. Continue on the road towards Les Mosses, and at the second hairpin bend take the small road left. If this is open you can often drive as far as Solepra, which is a chalet opposite the last chairlift of the Leysin ski area. Parking can be problematic at weekends. Later in the season you can drive right up to the col at Pierre du Moëllé.

Solepra. The choice of routes makes this area worth a couple of visits.

There may be a military presence at the Pierre du Moëllé. If so, just make it clear that you are going to stay on the southern side of the mountains. However, bombs will be going off in the distance making it seem like you have strayed into a war zone.

Route

From Le Sepey, just opposite the turn-off to Leysin, cross the bridge and take the path on the left signed to Pierre du Moëllé. This follows the river to emerge on the road half a kilometre before Solepra. From Solepra chalet leave the road to head diagonally towards the chalet above, just at the tree-line. Follow the summer path through the trees to the higher road (snowy), which leads up to the chalets at Pierre du Moëllé. Above, to the west, is lovely rolling terrain which takes you easily to the rounded hills of Les Chaux. Remember to look behind

The summit's ticked and everyone's happy! The Tour du Famelon

Further Options
From the col beneath the summit, Sur Treux is just to the south-east and is easily attained. NB On the 1:25,000 map this summit is not named – it is spot height 2194.

you at the Mont Blanc massif. From Les Chaux continue heading west, under a long rocky cliff, to climb more steeply up to a rounded ridge. Follow this ridge until you are forced around to the west side of the rocky summit. Wander through this undulating terrain then head up to the col at the south end of the summit. To climb the Tour de Famelon go steeply up the south-east slopes as far as you feel comfortable in snowshoes. Pick a flat spot next to rocks and leave snowshoes there, continuing on foot. A short rocky step is overcome by using a chain, which takes you to the summit.

Descend either by the same route, more or less, taking the best snow for the descent; or, from the col at the base of the south-east slopes, descend the slopes eastwards down a short wide gully. You are aiming for the pistes below, so search out the easiest slopes to get there. Be sure to head east not south. When you reach the pistes stay well to the edge and follow signs to Solepra.

At the base of the chairlift a piste leads across the river to the road. If descending to Le Sepey retrace your ascent route. To return to Pierre du Moëllé pick up the track from Les Fers around to the flat of La Badouse then walk back up to the col.

43: Monts Chevreuils, 1749m

Starting point	Military caserne 500m from La Lécherette
Starting altitude	1353m
Summit altitude	1750m
Altitude gain	397m
Time	3h round trip
Grade	1
Aspect	S
Map	1:25,000 Carte Nationale de la Suisse 1265 Les Mosses; 1:50,000 Carte Nationale de la Suisse 262 Rochers de Naye
Public transport	Bus Aigle–Les Mosses–La Lécherette

Access: From Aigle take the road to Les Mosses (also known as Col des Mosses) and continue to La Lécherette. Turn left at the entrance to the village and park just beyond the tank.

The Monts Chevreuils may be of modest altitude, but as a snowshoe outing they've got all the required ingredients: pleasant slopes, views, sunny aspect and plenty of alternative for route selection. Situated just north of the popular family ski resort of Les Mosses, the Monts Chevreuils are just on the edge of an area reserved for the army, but apart from a tank rather conspicuously guarding the car park you shouldn't see too much sign of military activity.

You would have to use your imagination to see Mont Blanc from here, but nevertheless views are spectacular. Usually the odd hot-air balloon will be seen bobbing along, coming from the nearby hot-air-balloon centre of Chateau d'Oex, and if you choose your day carefully

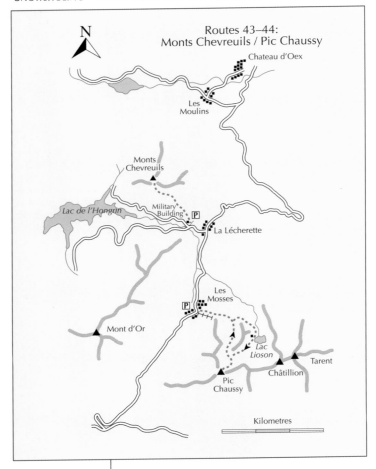

Routes 43–44:
Monts Chevreuils / Pic Chaussy

you'll enjoy the fabulous display of the Hot Air Festival which takes place the last week of January every year.

This walk can be done in any conditions. There are no steep slopes, and the route has frequent landmarks which are easy to find. A classic on snowshoes.

From the car park head up north to the road above, where there are several houses. This road is very often pisted for cross-country skiing, so be careful not to step on the tracks. Walk along the road westwards for a short distance to the large Sotanna farm building, which is before the trees where the road goes over a stream. Leave the road and take a north-westerly line to the obvious chalet above, at 1623m. Continue to the chalet in a col at 1720m between two small summits. The higher summit at 1749m is your objective, and it is reached by going below it for a short way west then ascending its south slope.

Descend either by the same route, or go along to the other summit at 1662m and then descend the enjoyable slopes south-east towards Les Téssailles and down to the car park.

Further Options

There are also two prepared snowshoe circuits at Les Mosses which can pleasantly fill an hour or so – see Route 44.

44: Pic Chaussy, 2351m

Starting point	Les Mosses
Starting altitude	1435m
Summit altitude	2351m
Altitude gain	916m
Time	5hrs
Grade	2
Aspect	NW, NE
Map	1:25,000 Carte Nationale de la Suisse 1245 Les Mosses; 1:50,000 Carte Nationale de la Suisse 262 Rochers de Naye
Public transport	Bus Aigle–Les Mosses

Access: From Aigle go up to Les Mosses (also know as Col des Mosses). Park at the bottom of the lifts at Les Fontaines.

This peak is relatively unusual as it features a cable car that is no longer functional. Unfortunately, although the pylons have been removed, the lift building at the top of the peak is still there and is rather an eyesore for the final

195

Further Options

Les Mosses has two waymarked walks for snowshoers. A plan is available from the Tourist Office, but they are easy to follow without it. One walk begins at the lift at the beginning of the Pic Chaussy walk and follows signs marked with a green TSL snowshoe in the vicinity of Lioson d'en Bas. The other starts further up the road at Arsat and follows waymarks of red TSL snowshoes. Both walks are about 2.5 to 3km long and take just over an hour. The latter walk can be accessed from Les Mosses by taking the pisted walking trail north towards La Lécherette.

slope. Nevertheless Pic Chaussy is still worth doing for its pleasant climb and superb panorama. From the summit you will enjoy views not only of the nearby peaks of Châtillon, Le Tarent and Mont d'Or, but also the imposing rocky Grand Muveran, Diablerets and the Mont Blanc massif.

Route

From the road head south-east, walking up next to the short lift. At the top of the lift go east and follow the gently angled forest track, which is often pisted, as far as the Liosan lake. Here you are likely to see hardy souls diving through holes cut in the ice – the idea seems to be to go in at one hole and out at another.

Traverse above the lake or, if the slopes are frozen too hard, walk across the lake (as long as it is also frozen). Pleasant undulating terrain follows as you head up to the all too obvious summit slopes, which are surprisingly steep and can be a bit icy after the passage of lots of ski tourers. Leave snowshoes next to the building which, despite being unattractive, does serve as a handy place to sit down. Continue on foot to the summit of Pic Chaussy.

Descend either by the same route or, after the steep slopes, turn left to descend the north face by Vers les Lacs. Continue on down to meet the ascent route above Lioson d'en Bas and return to the road.

Extensive views from Pic Chaussy (photo: Jon de Montjoye)

45: Pointe d'Arpille, 1982m

Starting point	Top of the Mazots chairlift
Starting altitude	1718m
Summit altitude	1982m
Altitude gain	375m
Time	3h30–4h30 round trip from the lift depending on whether you descend on foot or by lift to Les Diablerets
Grade	1
Aspect	NW
Map	1:25,000 Carte Nationale de la Suisse1285 Diablerets; 1:50,000 Carte Nationale de la Suisse 272 Saint Maurice
Public transport	Train Aigle–Diablerets

Access: From Aigle drive up to Le Sepey and over to Diablerets. Park in the village at the bottom of the Les Mazots chairlift.

There are many apparently quite insignificant hills in the Alps which, when ascended, give the most wonderful views, and the Pointe d'Arpille is certainly one of them. This walk presents no particular difficulties and is fairly safe in all snow conditions. The terrain is interesting and especially beautiful in the depths of winter, when the trees are laden with snow and animal tracks pattern the slopes. The big view from here is the Dents du Midi, whose steep slopes are particularly impressive from this vantage point, whilst the Culan provides a spectacular backdrop.

Route

At the top of the chairlift there is a restaurant on the ski piste called Les Mazots (this is not to be confused with the hamlet of the same name lower down). From the restaurant there is a superb view of the Pointe d'Arpille, with the impressive dark, rocky north face of Culan behind.

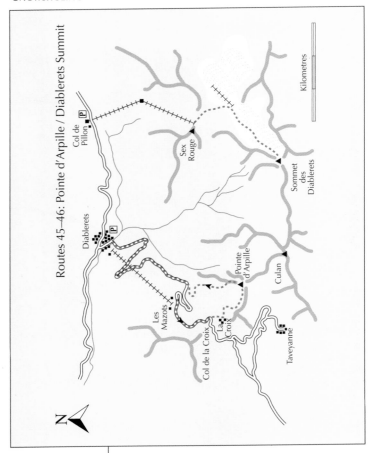

Routes 45–46: Pointe d'Arpille / Diablerets Summit

You will notice that a lot of people come up this lift with luges to descend the Col de la Croix road to Diablerets. Follow these lugers as far as the road then turn right and go up the road to the Col de la Croix, about 1.5km away. A cross-country ski piste arrives here from Villars, so be sure to keep off the piste once at the

col. Descend to pt 1732, and then walk south-west following a more or less horizontal track leading to the attractive hamlet of La Croix. There are fantastic views of the Dents du Midi from here. Continue on the same track, now slightly in descent and heading east towards,

The Pointe d'Arpille against a backdrop of rock and snow (photo: Jon de Montjoye)

199

Further Options The
Pointe d'Arpille can
be undertaken from
Villars by walking up
to the Col de la
Croix or making a
circuit via
Taveyanne, following
cross-country ski
pistes and coming
back onto the Col de
la Croix road at pt
1630. From here it is
a short walk up to pt
1732, then the route
can be followed as
described above.

but not as far as, the isolated building of Arpille. After
about 150m you reach a crossroads of tracks. Zigzag
south to pt 1902 then take the final rounded ridge,
wooded on the right, to the Pointe d'Arpille.

To descend, head down the bushy north ridge then
cut left off the ridge wherever looks best towards the
Arpille building. Before reaching it go down more gentle
slopes, still in a northerly direction, to pick up a very
obvious track curving north-north-east until gentle open
slopes are gained; these allow you to descend directly
onto a road, hitting trees again just above it. Turn left and
follow the road around to arrive in about 10 minutes
back on the Col de la Croix road just above pt 1543. With
good planning you would have a friend waiting
here with a sledge so as to whoop back down to Les
Diablerets, but if not either walk down or go back up the
track and take the lift down.

46: Diablerets Summit, 3210m

Access: From Aigle
drive over the Col de
la Croix down to
Diablerets then on
up to the Col de
Pillon. Park at the
car park for the
cable car.

Starting point	Sex Rouge, which is the summit of the two-stage Diablerets cable car
Starting altitude	2940m
Summit altitude	3210m
Altitude gain	270m
Time	3h round trip from the lift
Grade	G4
Aspect	N, E
Map	1:25,000 Carte Nationale de la Suisse 1285 Diablerets; 1:50,000 Carte Nationale de la Suisse 272 Saint Maurice
Public transport	Bus/train Aigle–Diablerets then bus to lift

Despite being very close to the Diablerets ski area, this
summit provides an interesting walk, with a potentially

awkward passage to gain the glacier. It is just far enough away from the lifts and gives a superb vantage point. Distant views of the Alps extend from the Mont Blanc massif to the Pennine Alps and to the Bernese Oberland. Whilst the angle of this glacier is very gentle, it is nevertheless glaciated and consequently the walk has a glacier grading. However, apart from the slight difficulty to attain the glacier, this is the easiest glacier walk in the guide. It should be remembered that when you take the cable car you are in a ski area, so you must respect the skiers and not obstruct the pistes.

Route

On emerging from the cable car you will find yourself surrounded by skiers. Stay well to the side as you head south-east down the ski run. The piste is steep at first, and the skiers will be going fast – so watch out. Once you have reached the flat Col de Tsanfleuron at 2848m trend round to the south following a natural line and climbing gently, staying to the right of the pistes, in the direction of Le Dôme. To gain the Glacier des Diablerets, and thus leave the bustle of the ski area, there are two alternatives, both starting at the top of the ski tow.

The first, and probably preferable, option is to follow the ridge of Le Dôme south-west over its summit and down to a col (which is under the letter 'a' of 'Diablerets' on the 1:25,000 map). From this point it is possible to drop steeply onto the glacier below. Crampons may well be needed for this short step.

The second, more awkward, option is from the top of the ski tow to traverse horizontally on the south-east side of Le Dôme to pass through a gap in the small hidden cliffs at about 2940m. Then walk up the true left bank of the glacier to arrive under the col mentioned in the first option.

From here, with no further difficulty, follow the true left bank of the glacier in a south-westerly direction to the Diablerets summit, finishing with a broad, easy but pleasantly airy ridge. Descend by the same route.

47: Col des Chamoix, 2660m

Access: From Aigle drive up to Villars and continue along past Arveyes, turning right at La Barboleusaz. Follow the Solalex road as far as it is snow-free, which in winter is usually up to Cergnement.

Starting point	Cergnement
Starting altitude	1290m
Summit altitude	2660m
Altitude gain	1370m (586m to the refuge Giacomini, 784m to the col)
Time	8h round trip (2h30 to hut)
Grade	To hut 1, to summit 2, if done in one day 2/3
Aspect	N, W
Map	1:25,000 Carte Nationale de la Suisse 1285 Les Diablerets; 1:50,000 Carte Nationale de la Suisse 272 St Maurice
Accommodation	Refuge Giacomini. Tel: 024 498 2295/024 481 3358
Public transport	Tram Aigle–Bex–La Barboleusaz

Anzeindaz is one of the mythical pastoral hiking areas of the Vaudoise Alps of Switzerland. An hour's walk from the popular hamlet of Solalex, dominated by the unique whaleback slabs of the Lion d'Argentine, Anzeindaz occupies a privileged position among spectacular limestone ramparts and knolls. Amongst the chalets here is the charming Refuge Giacomini, open for much of the winter, offering a warm welcome and a wealth of information on walking routes around the hut.

From the refuge there are a host of possibilities for the snowshoer, ranging from short strolls to more challenging outings. Surrounded by tempting snowy slopes and valleys, rounded summits and accessible cols, this is a dream location for a few days' snowshoeing.

The long route to Col des Chamois is an ambitious one-day objective, but becomes far more feasible when combined with a night in the refuge. Views are splendid throughout the walk, ever changing as you gain height

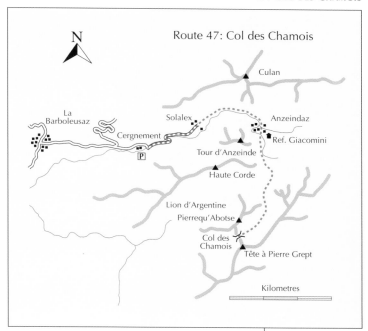

Route 47: Col des Chamois

N

Culan

La Barboleusaz

Solalex

Anzeindaz

Cergnement

Ref. Giacomini

Tour d'Anzeinde

P

Haute Corde

Lion d'Argentine

Pierrequ'Abotse

Col des Chamois

Tête à Pierre Grept

Kilometres

and new perspectives, to the final reward when you reach the hard-earned col and peer over the edge down into the Plan des Bouis valley far below. Ahead is the rocky summit of the Grand Muveran, whilst beyond are the Chablais peaks, often to be seen emerging from the sea of cloud over Lac Léman.

The walks in this area tend to be quite long, as there is a considerable distance on the flat to reach Solalex, so time should not be underestimated.

It is very important to note that there are steep slopes throughout this area that may well present a high risk of avalanche, notably in the Plan des Bouis valley. Consequently the Tour of the Lion d'Argentine mentioned in 'Further Options' is reserved for extremely stable snow conditions. The slopes of Culan to the north of

Anzeindaz also frequently avalanche. Note also that the terrain here is limestone, and there are areas of limestone pavement which need to be well filled with snow if you are to avoid falling into a crevasse.

Route

In the winter the road is used as a cross-country ski track, and this is also used by walkers as far as La Benjamine. From here a path heads up into the woods and makes its way very pleasantly to regain the road at the entrance to Solalex. There is usually a café open here. Continue up into the woods again, past the mysterious-looking cave of the Trou de l'Ours seen up on the right, and you will soon emerge into the delightfully open alpage of Anzeindaz. The Refuge Giacomini is easy to find.

Perched high above on a knoll is the Cabane Barraud, which is usually closed in the winter. Gentle and varied slopes lead south up into the more enclosed cwm formed by the summits of the Pierrequ'Abotse and the Tête Tsernou, with the Tête à Pierre Grept at the head. Continue up in the easiest line to reach the Col des Chamois. The final slopes are quite steep and can be challenging if the snow is hard windpack. Although marked as glacier on the map, this slope is in fact nevé. Descend by the same route.

Further Options The sky's the limit here on snowshoes: from the hut the Pas de Cheville, 2036m, is a good destination for a circular trip. It can be reached by going over the Roc de la Vache, then along the undulating terrain of the Hauts Crots to the Pas de Cheville and onwards to the Plan du Sex for good views over into Derborence. Return directly west from the col.

To the north-west of the hut is the accessible Tour d'Anzeindaz, 2170m, which can be ascended without problem from the hut. This can be combined with the summit of La Corde and a return via the Col des Essets, which makes for a more technical circuit. Finally, in very stable snow conditions, the Lion d'Argentine can be circumnavigated in two days with a night at the Refuge Giacomini.

Reach the Col des Essets from Les Plans sur Bex via Pont de
Nant and the alpage of La Vare, then return by Anzeindaz
and Solalex to Cergnement. Here take the track on the other
side of the river to Fratchi then continue on rolling terrain to
Sereussex. Descend the steep forest by the easiest way to
Les Plans sur Bex.

Solalex and the surrounding region has a series of snowshoe
trails signed by the TSL snowshoe logo. Information about
these can be obtained from Villars Tourist Office.

*En route for the Col
des Chamois*

SION/VISP REGION

Possible bases

Sion

Sion is at relatively lowly altitude, in the Rhône valley, but very central for the walks around here. It is a bustling town, but not unpleasantly so, and as long as you are willing to drive it could make a convenient base.

Ovronnaz

In a sunny position, with wonderful views, the only disadvantage with this choice is the winding access road, which you could travel a number of times during a week's walking. However, the village is pretty, with old chalets attesting to its history long before the ski lifts arrived. Good shops and restaurants offering regional specialities.

Vissoie/St Luc

There are many lodging possibilities along the length of the Val d'Anniviers. The first large village is Vissoie, more or less joined to St Luc. Whilst this is a ski resort, life is not dominated by skiing, and the emphasis is more on winter holidays than skiing itself. There are attractive old chalets and barns in Vissoie, as well as the usual shops and facilities.

Les Haudères

Again just one of many possible villages, this time situated at the head of the Val d'Herens. This is a traditional village, with tiny backstreets to explore, lined with ancient houses. The village is dominated by the mighty Dent Blanche that towers above.

Arolla

A tiny village with a surprising number of hotels and visitors, Arolla is really a small ski resort, but nevertheless could be used as a base for snowshoeing. It has a sense of tradition and the mountains around are stunning.

Zinal

At the end of the Val d'Anniviers is Zinal, a small town which is charming and practical at the same time. The old village preserves its traditional charm, whilst the main street has most necessary facilities.

Visp

Visp stands at the junction of the Rhône and Mattertal valleys, the latter splitting higher up, with the Saastal heading off to the southeast. It is a big town, probably too big to feel at home for a holiday.

Leukerbad

Nestled up against the towering cliffs of the Gemmi pass this is a town that welcomes all sorts of winter activities, as well as offering its famous spa baths. The Gemmi cable car gives access to the high Daubensee, where you are sure to find snow even in lean seasons. All facilities.

Zermatt

Not the best place to stay for snow-shoeing, but a really interesting small town with plenty going on. You would have to be willing to take the train each day down to Täsch then drive to walk areas, as the terrain around Zermatt doesn't really lend itself to snowshoe walks. There are other small towns in the Mattertal which could make a pleasant base, such as Saint Niklaus.

Fresh snow, good track

48: Dent de Morcles, 2969m

Access: From Martigny take the road towards Sion, leaving it at Riddes to head up the many switchbacks to the resort of Ovronnaz. Here, drive through the village to the chairlift car park.

Starting point	Ovronnaz
Starting altitude	1380m
Summit altitude	Col and Cabane de Fenestral 2453m, Dent de Morcles 2969m
Altitude gain	1073m to the col, 516m from col to summit
Time	4h from Ovronnaz to the col/cabane, 2h from col to summit. Descent 5h.
Grade	to col 1, to summit 2
Aspect	E, SE
Map	1:25,000 Carte Nationale de la Suisse 1305 Dent de Morcles; 1:50,000 Carte Nationale de la Suisse 272 St Maurice
Accommodation	Cabane de Fenestral. Belongs to Ski Club of Ovronnaz. Usually left open, no guardian except at busy times. Reservation is recommended. Tel: Tourist Office at Fully, 027 746 2080
Public transport	Bus Sion–Ovronnaz

Two huge rocky summits dominate the Rhône valley between Martigny and the Lac Léman: on the west side of the valley the well-known Dents de Midi, and on the east the far less famous Dent de Morcles. Whilst the west face of the Dent de Morcles is craggy, steep and imposing, the east face provides gentle and accessible terrain which make this summit a perfect snowshoe peak.

It is a summit from which the view is apparently endless – from Mont Blanc to the Matterhorn, to the nearby Dents du Midi, and to the far away Gran Paradiso and the hazy plains of Geneva.

Although the summit can be climbed in one day on

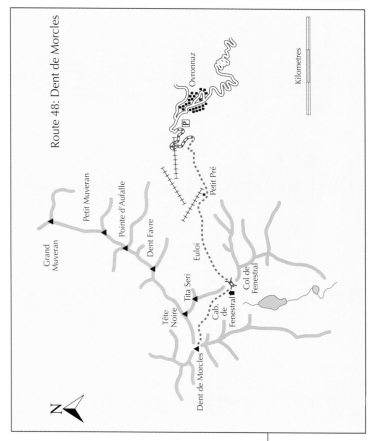

Route 48: Dent de Morcles

Kilometres

Ovronnaz

Petit Muveran

Pointe d'Aufalle

Dent Favre

Petit Pré

Grand Muveran

Euloi

Col de Fenestral

Tita Seri

Tête Noire

Cab. de Fenestral

Dent de Morcles

N

snowshoes it is a long way, and why rush such a beautiful walk? Better to take two days and spend the night at the well-appointed Cabane de Fenestral on the Col de Fenestral. If you just have one day, you could have a good walk just going to the col, which in itself gives spectacular views, including the Mont Blanc massif, and allows a taste of the splendour of this area.

The Dent de Morcles, seen in the background, is enjoyed by skiers and snowshoers alike

However, beware, this area features complicated terrain where fog could cause great problems of orientation, and the many steep slopes can be avalanche prone in high-risk conditions. Pick a period of settled weather with stable snow conditions.

Route

Described here is the ascent on foot from Ovronnaz. (It is possible, however, to gain a lot of altitude by using the chairlifts. If you want to do the summit in one day then it is essential to use the lifts. Take the Jorasse chairlift from the car park then walk down to the Col Express chairlift. From the top of the lift you will see the valley of Petit Pré a short distance below, where you can join the track going up to the col. Stay well to the side of the ski pistes as you descend – walkers are not officially allowed on the pistes. (Be aware that snowshoers are not always welcomed on the lift here.)

If you are not taking the lift from the car park follow

the road to the Sports Centre. From here there is a road (usually snowy) to Odonne. Instead of following this all the way take the shortcut straight up, marked as a footpath on the map. At Odonne a forest track leads up to Petit Pré. This will probably have been descended by skiers, and it passes very close to the ski pistes in two places. You will emerge from a narrow gully at the buildings of Petit Pré. This lovely sunny spot is a perfect place to break for a picnic.

There will be a good track from here, unless you've come immediately after fresh snow, in which case you should be extremely careful, as steep slopes threaten the rest of the walk.

Follow the valley up to the flat of Grand Pré, surrounded by the unusual rocky peaks of Tita Seri and the Dent Favre, then climb again up to the Col de Fenestral. Straight ahead in the distance is the Mont Blanc massif, with the Aiguille Verte and Les Drus looking particularly impressive. The Cabane de Fenestral is just below on the west side of the col.

To reach the summit, head back up to the col and take the rounded ridge leading past the cross. You will probably have to take off your snowshoes to traverse under a rocky buttress and possibly to continue on to regain the upper ridge. Be careful on this section, as the west slopes are steep and dangerous.

The track onwards leads under the west side of Tita Seri. Take the easiest line, which may not be where skiers have gone. On snowshoes you should aim for the flattest ground, even if it means losing height to gain it again later. Skiers often take a high traverse under the Tête Noire, but on snowshoes stay in the lower bowls which provide easy walking as you head north towards the summit. At about 2840m you will reach the edge of all things, where you can look down precipitous cliffs to the Glacier des Martinets far below. Here head west to reach the summit.

In foggy conditions none of this route is to be recommended, as it is very easy to get lost in this featureless terrain or inadvertently to step over the steep north or west faces of the Dent de Morcles.

Descend by the same route more or less, although you could vary the route from the summit, taking the best snow. Be careful regaining the hut, as the snow may have melted during the day and it could be slippery. Enjoy running down from the col, then plod on back to Ovronnaz and relax in the famed thermal baths.

49: Wildhorn, 3248m

Access: From Sion drive up through Ayent then onwards in the direction of the Lac de Tseuzier. After Pra Combère the road goes into a tunnel at Les Rousses. Park just before this tunnel.

Starting point	Les Rousses
Starting altitude	1767m
Summit altitude	Cabane des Audannes 2560m, Wildhorn 3248m
Altitude gain	793m to the hut, 688m hut to the summit
Time	3h30 to hut, 5h round trip hut to summit
Grade	G4
Aspect	E, N, S
Map	1:25,000 Carte Nationale de la Suisse 1286 St Leonard; 1:50,000 Carte Nationale de la Suisse 273 Montana
Accommodation	Cabane des Audannes. This hut is usually wardened only if there is a reservation. Tel: (guardian) 079 310 9060, (hut) 027 308 3186 or Tourist Office in Anzère, where they can make a reservation for you 027 399 2800.

Along with the Diablerets and the Wildstrubel, the Wildhorn completes the chain of peaks which form the western edge of the Bernese Oberland. These western outliers, although glaciated, are of more modest altitude than the major Oberland summits and are thus more accessible and appealing to the winter walker. The Wildhorn can be reached either from the Rhône valley

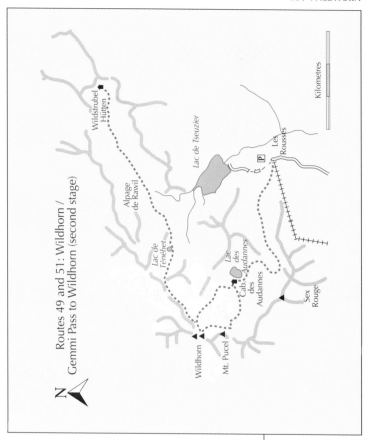

Routes 49 and 51: Wildhorn /
Gemmi Pass to Wildhorn (second stage)

by driving up to Les Rousses or from Lenk – this latter
start point is briefly described in 'Further Options', but is
outside of the area of this guidebook.

Whichever route is taken, the Wildhorn can only be
envisaged on snowshoes in very stable snow conditions.
The summer paths shown on the map above Les Rousses
should not be looked for, as they are not feasible in the

Gaston is a regular visitor at the Cabane des Audannes

Further Options The Wildhorn can be approached from Lenk via the Wildhorn hut. From Lenk go south following the road, which will be snowed-up, to Iffigenalp. Take the Iffigtal south-west to Groppi then onwards to Egge and up to pt 2086m. A slight descent leads to the lake, which can either be crossed if it is frozen or avoided by taking the northern shore. Follow the valley south-west under the northern slopes of the Schnidehorn (risk of avalanches) to the hut. From the hut go south-west to the Chilchligletscher then via an easy col to join the Glacier de Ténéhet, from where the summit is reached by gentle slopes going south-west.

snow. You must follow the lie of the land, staying in the valley rather than trying to take traverses. This means that the route follows what would be a very dangerous terrain trap in unstable avalanche conditions. As with all glaciated peaks crampons must be taken, and if the route is too steep or icy you should be prepared to turn back.

The Cabane des Audannes is in a wonderful position, circled on all sides by summits. If you are lucky, Gaston or one of his descendants will pop by in the evening to liven up your stay here.

The summit climb has some steep sections where it is possible that crampons will be more useful than snowshoes. This varies year by year, and you must be able to decide this for yourself. Your efforts will be rewarded by a splendid panorama encompassing the nearby Wildstrubel, the Oberland summits and the distant Pennine peaks on the far side of the Rhône valley. Away to the south-west the snowy tops of the Mont Blanc chain complete this visual feast.

Route

From Les Rousses head west up the valley. This is relatively gentle at first and takes you into the cwm of Les

Andins, bounded to the north by imposing slopes. Continue in the line of the valley west-south-west, where the cwm becomes steeper and narrow. Eventually the route emerges onto easier ground to the north-north-east of the Sex Rouge. Ignore all summer paths shown on the map. Ahead is the undulating plateau of Les Audannes, to the north-east of the Sex Rouge. Make your way by rolling terrain to the hut, which is found on the south-west side of the lake.

To gain the Glacier des Audannes from the hut several possibilities present themselves, the most obvious being either the steep cwm due north of the hut or the equally steep slopes to the east of Mont Pucel. Either way the snow may be hard and icy in the morning, so crampons could be needed.

Once attained, the glacier provides pleasantly angled slopes right up to the summit. The true summit is the left-hand one, although most people go for the rocky one on the right. You'll probably meet other people arriving on the summit ridge from the Wildhorn hut to the north-east. Descend by the same route.

50: Wildstrubel, 3243m

For awesome views the Wildstrubel can't be bettered. The vista that greets you on arrival at this summit stretches all the way from the Mont Blanc massif to the Bernese Oberland, and with its relative accessibility this summit gives a lot more than you have to put in to get there.

The Gemmi lift takes you high up to 2346m, from where you begin the walk with a short descent. On this first day flat strolling takes you almost to the Lammeren Hut, with just a short sharp pull at the end. The Lammeren Hütte, where you spend the night, is popular with skiers, so don't expect to be alone here, but sit out on the sunny terrace and enjoy the wonderful situation of this hut.

The next day the climb up to the summit is kind, with any steeper sections being generously interspersed

Access: From Sion drive to Sierre then onwards to turn off the main road at Leuk. Take the road north to Leukerbad. Follow signs to the carpark for the cable car at the top of town.

Starting point	Summit of Gemmi cable car
Starting altitude	2346m
Summit altitude	Hut 2501m, summit 3243m
Altitude gain	219m to the hut, 742m to the summit
Time	2h to hut, 4h round trip hut to summit
Grade	G4
Aspect	W
Map	1:25,000 Carte Nationale de la Suisse 1367 Gemmi; 1:50,000 Carte Nationale de la Suisse 263 Wildstrubel
Accommodation	Lammeren Hütte Tel: 027 470 2515, open mid-March to mid-May. However, the Gemmi lift closes mid-April.
Public transport	Bus Sion–Lenk–Leukerbad

Further Options

The Schwarzhorn is another possibility from here, but beware of the crevasses.

It is possible to approach the Lammeren Hütte from Kandersteg taking the Stock lift to Sunnbiel then coming up to the Daubensee via Schwarenbach. This is the way when the Gemmi lift is closed.

with gentle slopes to allow you to recover. In fact the Wildstrubel boasts three summits – all, unusually, exactly the same height. The direct route will take you to the Mittel Gipfel, and the Wildstrubel is to the left.

Route

From the cable car head down to the Lammerenboden, keeping clear of the ski pistes. Head along the flat towards the steeper slopes at the end of the cwm, where the steep walls can be breached by a more reasonable slope to reach the flat promontory where the Lammeren Hütte is placed.

The next day leave the hut heading almost due west. The slopes can be icy in the morning. If you are not happy, then wear crampons rather than snowshoes here. Round the end of the Lammerenhorn slopes and step onto the Wildstrubelgletscher. At this point you should rope up, as for all glacier travel.

Take the true left side of the glacier up relatively

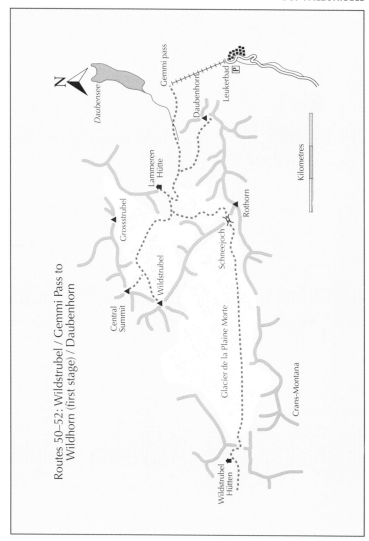

Routes 50–52: Wildstrubel / Gemmi Pass to Wildhorn (first stage) / Daubenhorn

The popular Lammeren Hütte provides a base for several peaks in the area

amenable ground. Before reaching the top decide whether to go to the Mittel Gipfel straight up above or the Wildstrubel. For the latter go up left to a col, the other side of which is impressively steep. Turn left to reach the summit. Descend by the same route.

51: Multi-Day Tour: Gemmi Pass, 2346m, to Wildhorn, 3248m

Starting point	Gemmi pass
Starting altitude	2346m
Finish altitude	Les Rousses 1767m
Time	4–6 days
Grade	G5
Aspect	All
Map	1:25,000 Carte Nationale de la Suisse 1267 Gemmi, 1266 Lenk, 1286 St Leonard; 1:50,000 Carte Nationale de la Suisse 263 Wildstrubel, 273 Montana
Accommodation	Lammerenhütte Tel: 027 470 2515, Wildstrubel Hütte Tel: 033 744 333, Cabane des Audannes Tel: (guardian) 079 310 9060, (hut) 027 308 3186 or Tourist Office in Anzère, where they can make a reservation for you 027 399 2800. All open Mid-March to mid-May, except Cabane des Audannes, which is subject to demand.
Public transport	Bus Sion–Leuk–Leukerbad. No transport to Les Rousses

Access: From Sion go to Sierre then continue towards Visp, turning off at Leuk to go north to Leukerbad.

In the spring, when snow conditions are stable, a multi-day hut-to-hut tour can be a very attractive proposition. However, to do such a trip on glaciers on snowshoes you must be experienced in glacier travel and you need to be sure that the weather forecast is good. Spring can soon revert to winter in the Alps, and the last thing you want is to get stuck in a hut when the snow conditions prevent a safe getaway.

This tour takes you into spectacular surroundings, among snowy peaks and impressive glaciers, with several possible snowshoe summits to tempt you along the way. It is four days long: Gemmi to Lammeren Hütte, Lammeren Hütte to Wildstrubel Hütte, Wildstrubel Hütte via the Wildhorn to Cabane des Audannes, then Cabane des Audannes to Les Rousses. Adding the Wildstrubel summit would make it five days.

Route

From the Gemmi pass head west to the Lammeren Hütte. This is described in the Wildstrubel ascent, Walk 50. It is possible to do the Daubenhorn en route (see Walk 52). A day could be spent doing the Wildstrubel, but do not be tempted to try to descend the south face of this summit, as it is too steep for snowshoes.

From the Lammeren Hütte go south to the Lammerengletscher and follow this up to the obvious col of the Sneejoch at 3020m. This is crossed, and west-facing slopes take you down onto the huge flat of the Glacier de la Plaine Morte. Hit this on a sunny afternoon and you'll probably understand how it got its name! Cross this, heading west to the steeper ground at the western end, bounded by the Weisshorn summit. This summit is adorned with military buildings and an associated cable car, none of which is on the map. The Wildstrubel hut is just beyond this summit, and is reached by skirting round the southern slope and ridge of the Weisshorn to a col (Weisshornlücke, 2904m), from where a short diagonal descent leads to the hut at 2793m.

The next long stage takes you over the Wildhorn and down to the Cabane des Audannes (see also map for Walks 49 and 51). Head down to the Rawilpass and enjoy the ease of the Rawil Alpage as far as the Plan des Roses at 2367m. (The Mittaghorn summit, 2686m, can be envisaged as a pleasant detour here.)

In favourable conditions it is possible from the Lac de Ténéhet to traverse south to the Col des Eaux Froides, 2648m, from where you'll see the Cabane des Audannes below next to the Lac des Audannes. However, you need to check out conditions for this traverse by calling the guardian of the Cabane des Audannes from the Wildstrubel hut the night before. If you were to go this way, you would ascend the Wildhorn the next day from the Cabanne des Audannes (see Walk 49).

Descend a little further, then leave the valley and cross the undulating lower south-eastern slopes of the Schnidehorn as far as the Lac de Ténéhet, 2440m. From here continue up the slopes ahead, which become steadily gentler as the summit of the Wildhorn is approached. Descend from the summit to the Cabane des Audannes (where you spend the night) by one of the two ways described in the Wildhorn route (Walk 49).

To descend the next day from Audannes take the undulating plateau of Les Audannes south-west towards the Sex Rouge. Under the northern slopes of this summit head east down steep ground into the cwm of Les Andins. Do not try to find any of the summer paths marked on the map as these are not feasible in the winter. Follow the bottom of the valley all the way down to Les Rousses.

52: Daubenhorn, 2941m

The Daubenhorn towers above Leukerbad, the winter resort nestled far below. It is a wonderful walking peak – high, with fine views – and its ascent is by slopes of just the right angle, not too steep, but steep enough to enable you to gain height quite quickly. Also popular with skiers, this summit is often climbed from the nearby Lammeren Hütte (see Wildstrubel, Route 50), and this is advisable later in the season when it is best to be on the top early in the day before the snow gets really soft in the afternoon heat.

The cable car from Leukerbad takes you up quickly to the Gemmi pass, an ancient smugglers' passage, with an improbably steep route from the village. You arrive to a world of ski pistes and all manner of activities – from sledging to snowboarding, cross-country skiing and walking. The Gemmi pass can be accessed from Kandersteg by groomed walking and skiing trails, so expect to find lots of people here.

The Daubenhorn is just above the pass, but the ascent route is via its north-western slopes, so you must

Access: From Sion go to Sierre then continue towards Visp, turning off at Lenk to go north to Leukerbad.

Starting point	Gemmi pass
Starting altitude	2346mm
Summit altitude	2941m
Altitude gain	650m .
Time	6h round trip
Grade	4 (3 without the summit scramble)
Aspect	N, W
Map	1:25,000 Carte Nationale de la Suisse 1267 Gemmi; 1:50,000 Carte Nationale de la Suisse 263 Wildstrubel
Accommodation	Lammeren Hütte Tel: 027 470 2515. Open mid-March to mid-May
Public transport	Bus Sion–Lenk–Leukerbad

head west along the flat Lammerenboden before heading up. The gentle slopes drop off very steeply to the north, so this would be a summit to avoid in fog, as it would not be wise to stray off route.

After some time climbing up in gentle curves, the final slope steepens up and a series of tight zigzags is required to ascend this. Look back and you'll see the whole of the Pennine range spread out before you, including the striking spire of the Matterhorn. If you peer carefully over the east face you will find the finish of a cabled *via ferrata* which provides an adventurous route to the top in the summer.

To reach the summit itself you must overcome a short scramble, and this requires a steady head or perhaps a rope. Certainly snowshoes must be removed for this part, following the ridge with a couple of teetering steps on rocky slabs before you gain the summit cross and a panorama that rivals any in the Alps: nearby the peaks of the area, dominated by the rounded summit of the Wildstrubel, and far off the Pennines and the Bernese Oberland.

The Daubenhorn, as seen from the Lammeren Hütte

Route

From the cable car head down to the Lammerenboden, keeping clear of the ski pistes. Head along the flat towards the steeper slopes at the end of the cwm. When you are level with the gentler slopes of the Daubenhorn start to head up these. Take the easiest line up, keeping away from the rocky northern slopes. A glacier is shown on the map, but this is now so small that it's dead and poses no threat in winter.

As the terrain steepens near the top make a series of zigzags. In hard or icy conditions it is feasible that you may have to remove snowshoes and use crampons to ascend the final section. When you arrive at the ridge at around 2850m you must certainly leave snowshoes here and continue on foot, perhaps using crampons and/or a rope according to conditions. If this final section seems rather more technical than you wished, then content yourselves with the lower high point – after all the views are still spectacular from here.

Descend by the same route. Be sure to get back to the Gemmi pass in time for the last lift. This peak could be combined with a continuation to the Lammeren Hut to do the Wildstrubel or with a traverse over to Kandersteg, from where transport can be taken back to Sion.

53: Pigne d'Arolla, 3796m

This summit is a must for anyone skiing the Chamonix Zermatt Haute Route and is also a heli-ski peak, so the chances of having a solitary experience here are minimal. Nevertheless, you won't regret a trip to this summit as long as you are well acclimatised to altitude and are sufficiently experienced and equipped to cope with the terrain and conditions. This peak is glaciated, and some of the slopes require skill in route-finding and seeing the best way through.

This is a two-day ascent, spending the night at the Cabane des Dix, magnificently positioned opposite the north face of the Mont Blanc de Cheilon. Of course the

Access: From Sion
drive up the Borgne
valley to Arolla.

Starting point	Arolla at the base of the ski pistes
Starting altitude	1956m
Summit altitude	Cabane des Dix 2928m, Pigne d'Arolla 3796m
Altitude gain	1012m to the hut, 936m to the summit
Time	4h to hut, 6–7h hut to summit to Arolla
Grade	G5
Aspect	N, W, E
Map	1:25,000 Carte Nationale de la Suisse 1347 Matterhorn, 1346 Chanrion; 1:50,000 Carte Nationale de la Suisse 5003 Mont Blanc Grand Combin
Accommodation	Cabane des Dix Tel: 027 281 1523. Open mid-March to mid-May
Public transport	Bus Sion–Arolla

views are great, and the Pigne d'Arolla is particularly special as you can do a traverse and come back via the Cabane des Vignettes, which makes a perfect place for an early lunch.

This route should not be underestimated – it is long and serious on snowshoes, despite the presence of lots of people, and you need to check that conditions are suitable before setting out.

Route

Ascend to the top of the first ski lift following the edge of the ski pistes. From here head west into the valley and up to the rocky Pas de Chèvres. Take a deep breath and carefully descend the ladders on the other side (obviously snowshoes should be attached to rucksacks here unless you're particularly nimble!). At the base of the ladders you have a choice of routes, depending on snow cover, to get down to the Glacier de Cheilon. If there is

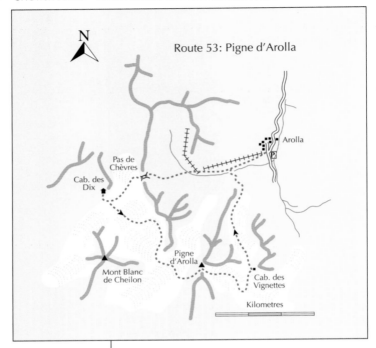

plenty of snow then you can descend directly to the glacier. However, if there are lots of boulders showing through the snowpack it is best to follow the summer path north-west to then zigzag back to the glacier under the loose moraine. Cross the Glacier de Cheilon towards the Cabane des Dix, visible on a rocky outcrop. To get up from the glacier to the Dix Hut, pass south of the hut's rocky perch and then climb up the steep slope to it.

The next day teeter back down this steep slope – you will almost certainly want to wear crampons for this in the early morning. You can probably put on your snowshoes when you reach the flat glacier. Remember to rope up. The glacier is crossed south-eastwards in the direction of pt 3029. Long before reaching this, trend up

*The Pigne d'Arolla
(photo: JP Ferlin)*

leftwards (north-east) then follow the fall-line of the glacier again south-east then south under the Pointes de
Tsena Refien. Remember to look up from time to time to
enjoy the dawn light on the nearby summits. As the glacier flattens out head south-west (in the direction of the
Col de la Serpentine) until it is possible to walk in a large
arc towards the Mur de la Serpentine, which is the steep
slope to the south. This section of the route is shown as a
dotted line on the ski map. This can be a straightforward
snow slope or a dome of blue ice – check with the
guardian before setting out, as the latter is not a pleasant
surprise. The slope is taken diagonally from bottom right
to top left (and for snowshoers will almost always be
taken on crampons) until the angle eases towards the
Col du Brenay. Contour around from the col and up to
the Pigne d'Arolla summit via a flat col which may well
be buzzing with helicopters dropping off their clients for
the ski descent.

Descend south-east. At about 3400m you will probably notice that a lot of ski tracks go off to the north to
take a shortcut – this is inadvisable on snowshoes as it
involves an icy traverse. Continue down in the same line

The exposed postion of the Cabane des Vignettes (photo: JP Ferlin)

towards the Col de Charmotane. As the ground flattens before the col itself turn left to cut under the lowest rocks and climb back up through a narrow col just west of pt 3162 onto a large flattish area. Head north to the Col des Vignettes, from where the hut is reached along an airy snowy and rocky ridge.

To descend from the hut walk north-east down the Glacier de Pièce. It is possible to avoid the steepening at 3000m by passing either right or left. However, below this point you should trend to the true left bank of the glacier, which is followed northwards under large crags until the snout of the glacier has been passed and you arrive in a small valley formed by a prominent moraine ridge on the left. From here either take the summer path, if the snow cover allows, or traverse around the moraines of the Glacier de Tsijiore Nouve and cut across onto the ski pistes, the edge of which can be followed down.

54: Col de Torrent, 2919m

Starting point	Villa
Starting altitude	1740m
Summit altitude	2919m
Altitude gain	1179m
Time	6–7h round trip.
Grade	2
Aspect	SW
Map	1:25,000 Carte Nationale de la Suisse 1327 Evolène; 1:50,000 Landskarte des Schweiz 5006 Matterhorn-Mischabel
Public transport	Bus Sion–Les Haudères–Villa

Access: From Sion drive south-west up the Val d'Herens to the attractive old village of Les Haudères. Turn left and take the smaller back road as far as Villa.

The Col de Torrent is situated on the ridge that divides the Val d'Herens from the smaller, wilder Val de Moiry, a tributary of the Val d'Anniviers. This has been a major summer crossing point for centuries, allowing passage in times past for traders and shepherds from one valley to the next, and nowadays used by hikers, especially those embarked on the Walkers' Chamonix–Zermatt route.

It is a long grind up to the col, but at any point this walk could be shortened and still provide a day out with fantastic views and lovely walking. Views to the east include the huge, unmistakable Grand Combin, Pigne d'Arolla and Mont Blanc de Cheilon. To the north across the Rhône valley are the Bernese Oberland Alps, including the Wildhorn and Diablerets.

However, those who persevere all the way to the pass will be rewarded with a fine panorama, even better in winter than in summer due to the clarity of winter skies. Ahead to the west are the some of the most beautiful high peaks of the Pennine Alps, including the Weisshorn, Bishorn and the Blanc de Moming. Below is the Moiry reservoir, often frozen in the winter. At the

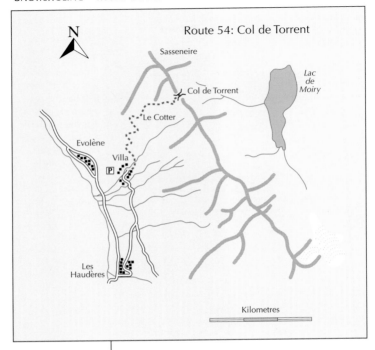

head of the Moiry valley the Moiry glacier comes tumbling down from the Grand Cornier and neighbouring peaks. Look back, and if you're lucky Mont Blanc will be shimmering in the background.

Route

From Villa head up behind the houses in a north-easterly direction. If there is no snow here follow the summer path; in snowy conditions take the easiest way. You must cross the Péterey torrent then continue up, all the time heading north-east. Several farm buildings are passed and the angle eases as you reach Le Cotter. Be sure to look behind you, as the views are magnificent. The col is fairly obvious above, reached by steeper slopes. Zigzag up to the col. (If you are in any doubt about the stability of the snow here then do not venture onto these final slopes.) Return by the same route.

55: Hotel Weisshorn, 2337m, and Bella Vouarda, 2748m

Starting point	Tignousa, at the top of the funicular
Starting altitude	2180m
Summit altitude	Hotel Weisshorn 2337m, Bella Vouarda 2748m
Altitude gain	157m to the hut, 411m to the summit
Time	1h30 hotel, 2h30 round trip hotel to summit
Grade	to hotel 1, to summit 2
Aspect	E, N
Map	1:25,000 Carte Nationale de la Suisse 1307 Saint Luc Vissoie Grimentz; 1:50,000 Landskarte des Schweiz 5006 Matterhorn Mischabel
Accommodation	Hotel Weisshorn Tel: 027 475 1106. Open Christmas to Easter. Reservations necessary.
Public transport	Bus Sierre–Vissoie–St Luc

Access: From Sion drive to Sierre then up the Val d'Anniviers to Vissoie. Here turn up left to take the hairpins to St Luc. Take the funicular to Tignousa.

The huge building of the Hotel Weisshorn towers domineeringly over the village of St Luc far below. Built in 1882, this was a classic establishment of that era, made for the rich tourists who came to the Alps for the views and traditional service. In 1991 the hotel was renovated, preserving its unique character, and it now provides excellent accommodation in an unforgettable setting.

Easily accessed from either St Luc or Chandolin, Hotel Weisshorn is a perfect starting point for various snowshoe forays into the surrounding mountains. Even if

The Hotel Weisshorn stands way above the Val d'Anniviers

the weather is doubtful, a night here is worthwhile for the atmosphere and sense of history. Given fine conditions, from this viewpoint you will see right across the Rhône valley to the Diablerets massif and the western Oberland peaks, notably the Wildhorn and the Wildstrubel, whilst at night the lights of Vissoie and St Luc twinkle far below.

Walking to the hotel is unusual, as you follow the Chemin Planètaire, which is a forest track, passable all winter, which has as its theme the solar planets. This is linked to the observatory set up by François-Xavier Bagnoud above St Luc at Tignousa. At intervals along the track there are large models of the planets. These are carefully placed at proportionately their true distance from the sun, which is situated at the start of this walk at Tignousa. Apart from the planets there are also fine views from this track as it traverses the hillside, in and out of

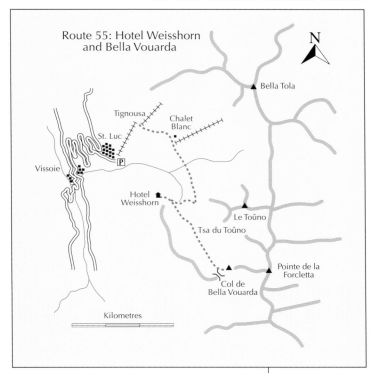

Route 55: Hotel Weisshorn
and Bella Vouarda

the forest. You'll soon spot the Hotel Weisshorn, perched right on the hillside seemingly miles away, but in fact you get there surprisingly easily.

Bella Vouarda is an attractive objective for the day after an overnight at Hotel Weisshorn, allowing plenty of time to descend to the valley afterwards. Reached by the Tsa du Toûno, a beautiful, gently rounded cwm and perfect for snowshoeing, the Bella Vouarda is the col at the head of the valley, but I suggest you go up left to the highpoint just above. It is possible to continue on to the Focletta col for views over into the Turtmanntal, but it is not really feasible to descend to this valley, as there is no

Further Options
Below are four
popular options.

• The walk to the
hotel can be
extended by starting
at Chandolin, thus
avoiding the funicu-
lar from St Luc and
making more of a
day of it.

• From Bella
Vouarda you can go
on to Forcletta,
which allows a peek
at the Turtmanntal
peaks, especially the
Brunegghorn and the
Weisshorn.

• The Meidpass can
be ascended, even
en route to the hotel,
by turning off from
the main track at the
Chalet Blanc and
heading east, staying
well clear of the ski
piste that descends
from the Pas de
Boeuf.

• From the signpost
in the Tsa du Toûno,
a left turn towards
the Lac du Toûno
leads to the Col
Vijivi, which allows
a glimpse into the
next valley.

accommodation in winter. Views make this walk very enjoyable, both to the south, where the Dent Blanche dominates, and north across the Rhône valley. The nearby Toûno is also an attractive backdrop.

Route

The Chemin Planètaire is signed from Tignousa. It takes a relatively flat line contouring the hillside way above the valley, with frequent and tempting glimpses of spectacular scenery from clearings in the trees. As you near the Hotel Weisshorn the trees thin and you can have no doubt where you are headed. Then the hotel vanishes for the last pull up from the Chalet Blanc.

Next day descend a little by the ascent path to go into the Tsa du Toûno valley. You will soon pass the building of Les Faches and from here it is advisable to stay on the left (east) of the streambed. This keeps you well clear of the steeper slopes coming down from the Pointes de Nava.

A signpost indicates the way left to the Lac du Toûno and to the right to Forcletta, which is the way you want. This almost flat paradise eventually gives way to slightly more demanding ground at a small lake at 2472m, which is passed on the left. It is then possible to weave up following the lie of the land to another flatter area. The col of Bella Vouarda is soon seen just below on the right, and you can gain the highest point above to the east.

Descend more or less by the same route, obviously taking the most enticing line for the descent. There are some nice little slopes here to bound down. If you are not returning to the hotel you can cut right (north-east) from Les Faches to rejoin the Chemin Planètaire just below. It is often possible to descend directly from the Hotel Weisshorn to St Luc by the forest footpath. This goes down to Le Prilet near the skating rink in St Luc and is marked on the ski piste map plan for St Luc. Check at the hotel that it is practicable.

56: Bishorn, 4153m

Starting point	Zinal
Starting altitude	1683m
Summit altitude	Hut 3256m, summit 4153m
Altitude gain	1576m to the hut, 897m to summit
Time	5h30 to hut, 4h30 round trip hut to summit
Grade	G4
Aspect	W, NW
Map	1:25,000 Carte Nationale de la Suisse 1327 Evolène, 1328 Randa; 1:50,000 Landskarte des Schweiz 5006 Matterhorn-Mischabel
Accommodation	Cabane de Tracuit Tel: 027 475 1500. Open late March to mid-May.
Public transport	Bus Sion–Zinal

Access: From Visp drive to Sierre and up the Val d'Anniviers to Zinal. Park at the far end of the village.

The Bishorn is an attractive summit not only in itself but also for its proximity to the mighty Weisshorn, from which it is separated by only a 120m height drop. From certain aspects it appears to be just a northern spur of the Weisshorn ridge system, but this view is dispelled when the Bishorn is seen from the north and its independence is evident.

The two-day ascent presents no technical difficulties beyond those normally associated with glaciated terrain, although care must be taken on the summit slopes as there are often cornices on the north side. However, the ascent to the Cabane de Tracuit, where you spend the night, is long and is inadvisable in unstable snow conditions. You need to wait for suitable conditions for this ascent, and it is worth calling the hut guardian for advice. Be sure to follow the way described below rather than the normal summer path.

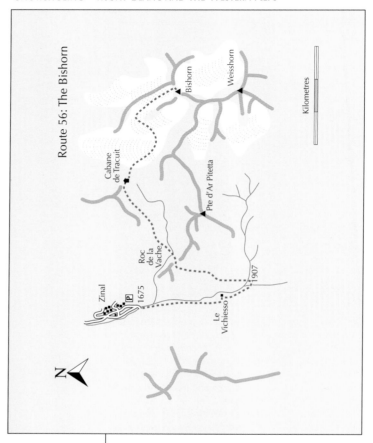

Route 56: The Bishorn

From the summit the views are splendid. Close by is the huge north face of the Weisshorn, sculpted by hanging glaciers and seracs. Further south the Zinalrothorn and the Obergabelhorn dominate the view. To the east is the Brunegghorn and to the north, glimpsed through the Turtmanntal, are the Oberland peaks, including the shapely Blümlisalphorn.

Before setting off for the hut, or afterwards, having enjoyed well-earned refreshments in Zinal, take a stroll along the back road of the village, where there are many old, well-preserved chalets, testament to the long and active history of Zinal.

Glacier walking

Route

From the south end of town head along the valley going south. Cross the bridge at pt 1675 and follow the true left bank of the Navisence river for about 3km. You will pass the buildings at Le Vichiesso. Cross back over the river at the bridges at pt 1907. Head up north across the slopes of Ar Pitetta and Tsijière de la Vatse to gain a little col to the south-east of the Roc de la Vache, 2581m. From here a slight descent gains the Torrent du Barmé, which is crossed. The Cabane de Tracuit is visible above but there's still a way to go. Go up past the alpage of Combautanna, 2578m, then head east-north-east and reach the Col de Tracuit by a long ramp. The hut is to be found just to the right of the col, on a rocky platform above the Turtmann Glacier. From here you have perfect views of the next day's objective.

From the hut take an easterly line over the Turtmann Glacier to its eastern branch. Be careful not to go north-east here, where there are often cornices. Take the north-west face all the way up to the col between the two summits of the Bishorn and turn right to go up the summit ridge to the higher top. Descend by the same route.

57: Breithorn, 4164m

Access: From Visp drive up the Mattertal to Täsch. Cars are not allowed beyond this point, so take the train to Zermatt.

Starting point	Top of Klein Matterhorn lift
Starting altitude	3883m
Summit altitude	4164m
Altitude gain	368m
Time	3–4h round trip from lift
Grade	G4
Aspect	SSW
Map	1:25,000 Carte Nationale de la Suisse 1348 Zermatt; 1:50,000 Landskarte des Schweiz 5006 Matterhorn-Mischabel
Public transport	Train Visp–Zermatt

From the Mattertal valley the Breithorn appears as a huge, complex mass of rock and snow, dominating the western end of the Monte Rosa group of peaks. Dwarfed beside this summit is the insignificant-looking Klein Matterhorn, 3883m, summit of the cable car out of Zermatt. This lift allows the Breithorn summit to claim its place as one of the most accessible 4000m peaks in the Alps.

However, this summit should not be underestimated. At this altitude you will certainly feel the effects of the thinner air, which make this ascent seem much harder than it would lower down. The Breithorn is usually quite popular, but don't be fooled into thinking there are no dangers – the area is glaciated and there is at least one bergschrund waiting for unsuspecting unroped climbers.

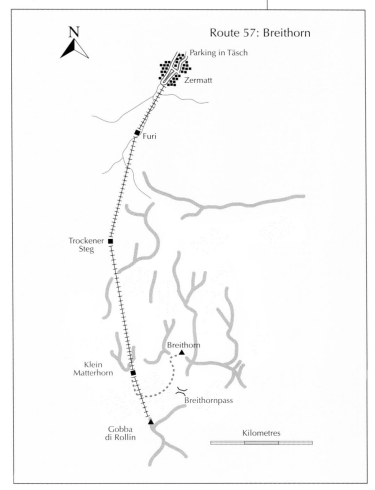

N

Route 57: Breithorn

Parking in Täsch

Zermatt

Furi

Trockener Steg

Breithorn

Klein Matterhorn

Breithornpass

Gobba di Rollin

Kilometres

Crevasses are preferably to be viewed from above

Views from the summit are quite simply superb – you are right in the midst of the Zermatt peaks – the Matterhorn, Castor, Pollux, Lyskamm and Monte Rosa. More distant views include the Mont Blanc massif, the Gran Paradiso and the Saas Fee peaks of the Täschhorn, Dom, Alphubel … the list is almost endless.

Route
From the Klein Matterhorn lift station walk through the tunnel and very slightly down following the line of the ski tow to the wide col at 3796m. Head east-north-east at first towards the Briethornpass, then curve leftwards in a large arc, without going to the pass itself, towards the increasingly steep south-west summit slopes to reach the broad south-west ridge. This leads easily to the summit, but beware of the steep drop-off down the north face. Descend by the same route.

ITALY
Aosta Region

Aosta
This is a large town with lots of history, definitely worth a visit even if you don't stay there. It is near many of the walking areas and, with Italian hospitality guaranteed, it's a big town that could make a good base for a holiday.

Courmayeur
Situated right under Mont Blanc, Courmayeur is the Italian equivalent of Chamonix. However, it's considerably smaller than its French counterpart and this adds to its charm. The town centre features several rather chic shops, a fine church, and interesting alleys and small streets to amble through.

Cogne
This small town is very popular in high season and justifiably so, as it is charming and traditionally Valdotain (Val d'Aosta). Here you'll find good food and a warm welcome, but, in the holidays, lots of people too. There is only minimal ski lift development in the Gran Paradiso National Park, which makes it a pleasant place to walk.

Pont
Pont is a hamlet featuring several hotels, only one of which is actually at Pont itself. It is a good choice if you want to be somewhere away from it all, right in the heart of the Gran Paradiso park.

Looking north from the Col Serena (Route 58)

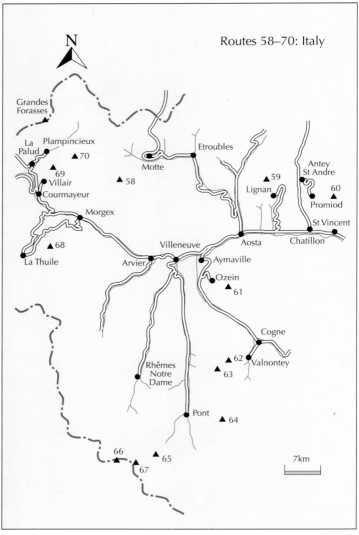

N

Routes 58–70: Italy

Grandes
Forasses

La
Palud   Plampincieux
        ▲70
        ▲
    ▲ 69
    Villair
Courmayeur

Etroubles

Motte

▲ 58

Lignan   ▲ 59

Antey
St Andre
        ▲ 60
Promiod

Morgex

▲ 68

Villeneuve

Aosta

St Vincent
Chatillon

La Thuile

Arvier

Aymaville

Ozein
▲ 61

Cogne

▲ 62
Valnontey
▲
63

Rhêmes
Notre
Dame

Pont

▲ 64

66
▲   ▲ 65
67

7km

Near to Helbronner above Courmayeur

58: Col Serena, 2547m

Access: From Aosta drive up towards the Grand St Bernard Tunnel. Just before the toll station take a road on the right which goes to the small Crevacol ski resort. Park as for the ski lifts.

Starting point	Crevacol ski resort car park – Motte
Starting altitude	1660m
Summit altitude	2547m
Altitude gain	887m
Time	4h30–5h round trip
Grade	2
Aspect	N
Map	1:25,000 Carte Nationale de la Suisse 1365 Gd St Bernard; 1:50,000 IGC 4 Monte Bianco
Public transport	Bus Aosta–Etroubles–Crevacol ski area

As a change from summits, sometimes a col can provide a good objective for a snowshoe walk, if the views are good and the terrain pleasant. The Col Serena is a beautiful setting in winter, with its lower forests and its gentle upper slopes with steeper summits all around, but not towering too close, so that the col itself remains open and spacious.

The best views are behind, of the broad, rounded summit of Mont Velan and, as you gain altitude, the Grand Combin, and this vista is especially to be savoured during the descent. There's also plenty to please the eye during the ascent, especially the attractive tumbledown farm buildings at Alpe di Bois, where the old roofs are typical of Valdotain (Aosta valley) architecture.

Facing north-east, this walk often keeps light cold snow, which is a joy to descend. However, immediately after heavy snowfall care must be taken, as the slopes to the sides are steep and prone to avalanche.

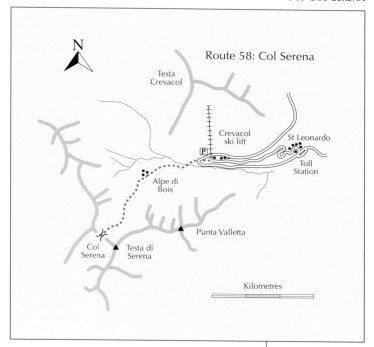

Route 58: Col Serena

Testa
Crevacol

Crevacol
ski lift

St Leonardo

P

Toll
Station

Alpe di
Bois

Punta Valletta

Col
Serena

Testa di
Serena

Kilometres

Route

From the car park walk along the dirt road to the houses at Ponti then head up into the forest, following the trail. Take the lower path, which leads through the trees to the ruins at Alpe di Bois. Continue on up in a south-westerly direction, alternating between relatively flat and steeper sections, to reach the col.

Return by the same route, although with a bit of imagination you willl almost feel as though you've done a circuit if you choose different slopes for the return trip.

Further Options It is possible to go over the col and down to the Aosta valley, but in most cases this would cause all sorts of complications with transport.

59: Monte Morion, 2709m

Access: From Aosta take the road to Nus. In the town turn left following signs to the Saint Bartélemy valley. The small road winds up the valley to the attractive village of Lignan, where there is a small ski station. Park opposite the church

Starting point	Lignan
Starting altitude	1633m
Summit altitude	2709m
Altitude gain	1076m
Time	6h round trip
Grade	2
Aspect	S
Map	1:25,000 IGC 115 La Valpelline; 1:50,000 IGC 5 Cervino Matterhorn e Monte Rosa

The village of Lignan is perched in the most perfect position, with sun all day long and a view to die for: the peaks of the Gran Paradiso range, with Mont Emilius and Grivola taking prime position. Even though the new observatory building is a bit space-age with its shiny dome, the village is a beautiful place to linger.

Monte Morion benefits from the same vista, but it gets even better, and you can add in the Mont Blanc massif, Monte Rosa and the whole of the Aosta valley spread out below. The summit is not difficult, and the way is very pleasant once you've got through the initial slopes which are taken up by ski pistes. This is not a major resort, though, and you shouldn't have any problem walking next to the pistes.

Route

Go up past the observatory building, keeping off the ski pistes as best as possible. Your objective is the top of the drag lift over on the left. Above the lift are a couple of smartly renovated buildings, and next to these is a signpost which directs route number 11 Col Oratoire Cuney to the right. This is our route for the moment, so go right and up, keeping well right of the trees to a partly renovated farm building on the edge of the forest. Go steeply up (north) into the woods. When the angle eases head rightwards around the hillside to reach a clearing. Ahead you can see the old tumbledown houses of Alpe Fontaney at 2079m. Go along to these then beyond, behind the second house, in the same direction for about 5 minutes on a big wide track. A sign directs you up the hill (north again), but this sign may not be visible in the snow. It is more or less where the wide track becomes flat.

This climb takes you above the tree-line, and you can clearly see Monte Morion above and to the right. However don't go there directly – head up north towards

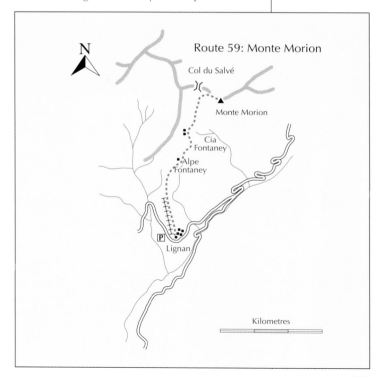

Route 59: Monte Morion

Lignan, starting point for Monte Morion, with Mont Emilius behind

the steeper slopes under pt 2656 and you'll find the farms of Cià Fontenay, 2302m. Ahead is the Col du Salvé and behind are the summits of Monte Pisonet and the Becca de Merlo.

Take the easiest ground to reach the rounded western slopes of Monte Morion and onwards to the top. Return by the same route.

60: Monte Zerbion, 2719m

This summit is little known outside the Val d'Aosta, yet it really is a classic. Starting in the sleepy village of Promiod, basking in the sun, you meander up into the forest, passing summer farms, to emerge onto a broad, rounded shoulder high above the valley. Far below is the town of St Vincent, whilst in all directions are rocky spires, snaking glaciers and ice-cream-topped snowy summits – Mont Blanc, the Matterhorn, Grivola, Monte Emilius … you name it, it's there.

From the subsidiary summit at pt 2381 (not marked

Starting point	Promiod
Starting altitude	1492m
Summit altitude	2719m
Altitude gain	1227m
Time	6–7h round trip
Grade	3
Aspect	W
Map	1:25,000 no map found; 1:50,000 IGC 5 Cervino Matterhorn e Monte Rosa

Access: From Aosta take the motorway to Châtillon. Exit here and go up the Cervinia valley as far as Antey St André, where you take the right turn to Promiod. Park at the entrance to the village.

on the Italian map but obvious when you get there) things become a bit more serious, as an impressive ridge holds the key to the summit of Zerbion. This requires care and sometimes may not be a feasible proposition. Once again, turning back may be the sensible thing to do, and if so content yourself with the lower high point – after all the panorama is pretty good. The ridge tends to have a cornice on the left side, and this means you have to walk on the right-hand slopes. In fresh snow it's possible that these slopes could be avalanche prone. In lean snow conditions there may be ice on the slopes, in which case crampons may be necessary. There are also a couple of steep sections which can seem rather more intimidating on the descent when your gaze is drawn to the distant valley.

The summit is guarded by a larger than life Madonna, poised behind an altar, and in summer mass is held here on special occasions.

Route

Walk through the village and follow the ancient mule track marked by yellow waymarks up the hillside. This leads onto a wide track which goes up the Promiod valley. At about 1700m the track goes over the river and up into the forest past the Arsine farm building. Continue on the track, which makes a rising traverse rightwards to open slopes leading up to the Francou alpage. Here turn

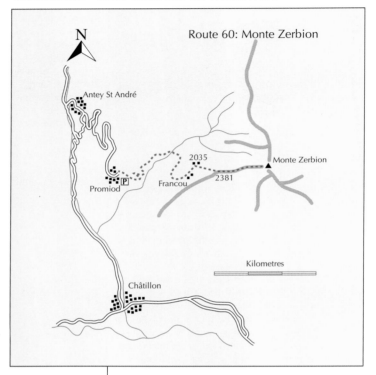

left (note: the map shows the path going right here) and go along a few metres to the other buildings, from where you head directly up into the forest (east). There are a signpost and yellow waymarks if the snow isn't hiding them.

Coming out of the forest you will see the Madonna on the summit and a series of large stones marking the way onwards. The small summit at 2381m is a good place to stop and assess whether the summit ridge is appealing or not.

To reach the Monte Zerbion summit you will have to leave your snowshoes at some point and continue on

foot. Be extremely careful not to step onto the cornice on this arête – it's not easy to see where it starts, and other tracks do not necessarily mean it is safe. At the top enjoy a 360° panorama, including the Monte Rosa massif, which is seen behind the pedestal. Return by the same route.

The snowy summit arête of Monte Zerbion, capped by its Madonna

61: Pointe de la Pierre, 2653m, and Pointe del Drinc, 2663m

The Gran Paradiso massif is penetrated by several long valleys and the Cogne valley is one of them, shooting up from the huge axis of the Aosta plain. The Pointe de la Pierre and its close companion the Pointe del Drinc stand above this junction, like guardians surveying all that goes on below. It is not difficult to imagine that these twin summits command one of the best panoramic views that can be had. If you can't see it from here, it's not worth seeing!

The route is quite long, and unless you shortcut the forest track it is even longer, but the upper slopes make it

Access: From Aosta take the road to Aymavilles and on in the direction of the Cogne valley. After a few kilometres a left turn takes you up to the village of Ozein. Go through the village and park on the road a little way beyond, where a forest track goes off right, signed to the Alpes of Romperein and Pierre amongst others.

Starting point	Ozein
Starting altitude	1370m
Summit altitude	2653m and 2663m
Altitude gain	1283m (1293m)
Time	7h round trip
Grade	2
Aspect	W
Map	1:25,000 no map found; 1:50,000 IGC 3 Gran Paradiso

all worthwhile, and the final rounded crest that takes you to the strange summit post of the Pointe del Drinc is a place to linger and to store up memories for those grey days back home when blue skies and snowy slopes seem just a distant dream.

Route

Walk along the forest track. Whenever you feel the urge, shortcut up between the long bends, as these do add a lot of distance to the walk. However, the shortcuts are steep, so don't overdo it. When you reach a clearing and the buildings at Alpe Champchenille, which are the first buildings you'll see and are not marked on all maps,

Nearing the top of the Pointe de la Pierre, with Grivola in the background

252

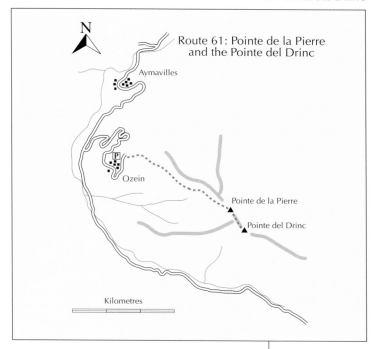

head south-east straight uphill. You'll soon be back in the woods, and can pick the easiest way winding between the larch and spruce trees. After some altitude gain arrive once more on the track at around 1900m near the buildings of Bardoney, which are in a fine position at a bend in the track directly opposite the spectacular soaring peak of Grivola and its neighbours.

Here you can again go directly up and will soon leave the trees. Ahead the Pointe de la Pierre is obvious. The best way is to head up towards the ridge on the left and follow this, to avoid making an ankle-jarring diagonal traverse across the south-west slopes. When you reach the shoulder you'll see the ski lifts of Pila below and may meet people coming up from this direction.

The Pointe de la Pierre is soon attained; for some this is enough, though you can go on a little way to the Pointe del Drinc – it is a few metres of descent then a short climb up, probably leaving snowshoes in the col between. It is worth doing this if you have time, as you get to see everything there is to see.

Return by the same route, perhaps loping down the south-west slopes a little way if the snow is stable and tempts you.

62: *Rifugio Vittorio Sella, 2584m*

Access: From Aosta drive towards Courmayeur a little way before turning off at Aymavilles up the valley to Cogne. Here turn right and go up to Valnontey, which is the end of the road.

Starting point	Valnontey car park
Starting altitude	1666m
Summit altitude	2584m
Altitude gain	918m
Time	5h round trip, but the animals and the food could change this dramatically.
Grade	2
Aspect	E
Map	1:25,000 IGC 101 Gran Paradiso; 1:50,000 Kompass Carta Turistica 86 Gran Paradiso
Accommodation	Rifugio Vittorio Sella Tel: 0165 74310. Open mid-March to mid-May.
Public transport	Bus Aosta–Cogne

The Gran Paradiso is literally a paradise for alpine fauna. This is no less true in winter, when you'll see lots of chamois grazing near the road and almost certainly groups of ibex in the woods. Do respect their space and use binoculars rather than getting too close, although, having said that, sometimes you almost have to nudge the ibex off the path.

Rifugio Vittorio Sella is in a fine position, above the

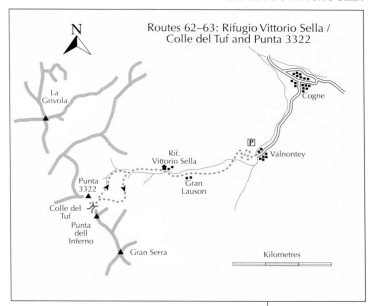

Routes 62–63: Rifugio Vittorio Sella /
Colle del Tuf and Punta 3322

N

La
Grivola

Cogne

Rif.
Vittorio Sella

P   Valnontey

Punta
3322

Gran
Lauson

Colle del
Tuf

Punta
dell
Inferno

Gran Serra

Kilometres

Valnontey valley, surrounded by rocky peaks and narrow
cols. There will probably be skiers returning from their
morning ski tours, which provides entertainment as they
swoop, with varying degrees of elegance, back to the
hut. Be sure to go into the refuge, where you will be
warmly welcomed, and you can enjoy a superb Italian
lunch before wobbling back down the hill to Valnontey.

   This walk provides superb views of the surrounding
peaks above Valnontey, as well as superb examples of
Valdotain (valley of Aosta) architecture, both old and
new. The roofs of heavy slate are particularly fine.

Route
Take the wide path, which is well signed, out of Valnontey
village. The main trail up to the Vittorio Sella refuge was
closed in summer 2002. The way has been redirected
after about 40 minutes to turn off left across a bridge over

Ibex on the slopes above Valnontey

the river which gushes down from the mountains above. Beyond is a narrow wooded area. Traverse out of this onto quite steep slopes which are cut through by lateral rocky ridges. If you haven't already put on your snow-shoes, you can expect to do so here at the remains of an old farm. Ascend these slopes to pass more ruins, then continue on gentler terrain to the newly restored farm at Gran Lauson, 2495m. Carry on up behind the farm rather than taking the summer path down and over the river.

Rifugio Vittorio Sella is to be found about 15 minutes from here, although the first building you see is not the hut but a National Park house. Return by the same route.

63: Colle del Tuf, 3255m, and Punta 3322

Access: From Aosta drive towards Courmayeur a little way before turning off at Aymavilles up the valley to Cogne. Here turn right and go up to Valnontey, at the end of the road. Take the trail up to Rifugio Vittorio Sella as described in Route 62.

The Colle del Tuf is accessed from the superb Rifugio Vittorio Sella and provides a good reason to spend the night there. Early in the morning the east slopes of the Punta del Tuf and the Punta dell'Inferno are bathed in an orange glow which makes the early start almost acceptable.

From the col you will be rewarded with fine views of the Grivola, whilst on the far side of the Valnontey valley a whole chain of snowy peaks, too numerous to denote here, will certainly complete this fine vista.

A circuit is described here, but the descent could be used for the ascent if preferred. Although a glacier is shown on the map under the col, this is very small and is avoided by this route.

Starting point	Rifugio Vittorio Sella
Starting altitude	2584m
Summit altitude	3322m
Altitude gain	738m
Time	4h round trip from the hut
Grade	3
Aspect	E, N
Map	1:25,000 IGC 101Gran Paradiso; 1:50,000 Kompass Carta Turistica 86 Gran Paradiso
Accommodation	Rifugio Vittorio Sella Tel: 0165 74310. Open mid-March to mid-May.
Public transport	Bus Aosta–Cogne–Valnontey

Route

Leave the Rifugio Vittorio Sella (see Route 62) heading westwards to enter a little gorge just above. Immediately turn left (south) up a subsidiary gorge heading towards the obvious yellow cliffs above. Climb steeply rightwards to gain the large cwm to the west of the cliffs. (If there is insufficient snow in the subsidiary gorge go on up the main gorge until it is possible to walk up into the cwm.)

Follow undulating terrain towards, and then up into, a broad gully that leads to a col on the Costa Verda ridge, which separates this cwm from the next one. Climb the gully, or the terrain to the left, then head up steep rocky ground or the snow slope to the right, depending on the snow cover, to reach the Colle del Tuf, 3255m (beware of wind slabs directly below the col). The Punta 3322 is just nearby to the north and makes a nice summit, as does the summit to the left (south) side of the col, the Punta dell'Inferno, 3393m.

To return, redescend to the col and continue down to the west of the Costa Verda ridge until a large flat is gained. Turn east and follow the bed of the valley directly to the refuge.

64: Rifugio Vittorio Emanuele, 2732m, and Gran Paradiso, 4061m

Access: From Aosta drive towards Courmayeur a little way before turning off at Villeneuve. Go up through the interesting village of Introd, then on up the Valsavarenche to the end of the road at Pont.

Starting point	Pont
Starting altitude	1960m
Summit altitude	Rifugio Vittorio Emanuele 2732m, Gran Paradiso 4061m
Altitude gain	772m to the hut, 1329m to the summit
Time	2h30 to hut, 8h round trip hut to hut
Grade	to hut 2, to summit G4
Aspect	W
Map	1:25,000 IGC 101 Gran Paradiso; 1:50,000 Kompass Carta Turistica 86 Gran Paradiso
Accommodation	Rifugio Vittorio Emanuele Tel: 0165 95710. Open mid-March to mid-May
Public transport	Bus Aosta–Pont

The Gran Paradiso is one of the most amenable alpine peaks that attain the sought-after 4000m height. It is not only the highest peak in this range, but also the highest wholly in Italy, and provides fabulous views of the neighbouring massifs including Mont Blanc, Monte Rosa, the Matterhorn, Monte Viso ... the list goes on and on.

It is justifiably popular, especially in winter with ski tourers and snowboarders, the latter usually ascending on snowshoes. The ascent takes two days, with a night at the Rifugio Vittorio Emanuele. The refuge gets busy in the season and reservations are essential. Despite the people, it makes a really fine summit on snowshoes, as the glacier is not too steep or crevassed, although – as with all glacier travel – roping up is not optional. The rocky scramble to the summit and the waiting Madonna provides a piquant finale to an unforgettable expedition.

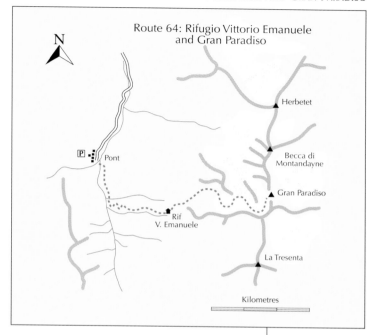

Route 64: Rifugio Vittorio Emanuele
and Gran Paradiso

N

Herbetet

P Pont

Becca di
Montandayne

Gran Paradiso

Rif
V. Emanuele

La Tresenta

Kilometres

Route

From Pont cross the bridge over the river and follow the
track along the true right bank of the Torrent Savara until
you find the trail that goes up east into the larch trees.
This old mule track will probably be snowy, but you can
usually see where it goes. It is followed in a long series of
zigzags up through the forest and onwards above the
tree-line. In icy conditions crampons may be more
appropriate than snowshoes. The terrain finally eases
and the strange-shaped hut is soon found under the
western slopes of the Gran Paradiso and its neighbours
La Tresenta and Ciarforon.

The next day make your way around the west ridge
of the Becca di Montcorvé to reach the Gran Paradiso
glacier, which is followed up to the Col di Becca di

259

A social day on the Gran Paradiso (photo: JP Ferlin)

Montcorvé. You may well meet people here coming up the adjoining glacier on the left from the Rifugio Federico Chabod. The slopes steepen (crampons will probably be required), and you go up north to the col at Il Roc, 4026m. Views here are spectacular down the other side of the range towards Valnontey and way beyond. From here to the summit is scrambling terrain, so you can certainly leave snowshoes behind. Keep the rope on, though, as a fall from here would not be good. An exposed traverse provides some excitement, but hurry onwards to the security of the Madonna on the summit. To descend, take a deep breath and return by the same route.

65: Colle del Nivolé, 2612m

The Colle del Nivolé is perhaps a strange choice of objective in some ways as it is on a summer road. However, it makes a great walk for: the terrain passed through to reach it; the views, firstly of the Gran Paradiso

Starting point	Pont
Starting altitude	1960m
Summit altitude	2612m
Altitude gain	652m
Time	6h round trip
Grade	2
Aspect	NE
Map	1:25,000 IGC 102 Valsavarenche; 1:50,000 Kompass Carta Turistica 86 Gran Paradiso
Accommodation	Rifugio Chivasso Tel: 1024 85150. Open mid-March to mid-May
Public transport	Bus Aosta–Pont

Access: From Aosta drive towards Courmayeur a little way before turning off at Villeneuve. Go up through the interesting village of Introd then on up the Valsavarenche to the end of the road at Pont.

range then, from the col, of all the Val d'Aosta and the Piedmont Alps; and for the animals living in the area.

The walk is quite long, despite the relatively modest height gain, as a lot of distance is covered. It could be shortened before the col and still be a very pleasant outing. This walk should not be envisaged too early in the season when the snow may be unstable, as there is a risk of avalanche in certain places.

The Rifugio Chivasso is open in late winter and would provide shelter in bad weather or a refreshment stop.

Route

From Pont a signpost behind the restaurant marks the way into the woods, along the true right bank of the river. The trail soon steepens and climbs in zigzags up to the Croix de Arolley at 2310m. Turn around and enjoy beautiful views of the Gran Paradiso, flanked by the Piccolo Paradiso on one side and Tresenta and Ciarforon on the other.

Now easy walking leads into the flat-bottomed Nivolé valley. However, beware the steep slopes to either side – this is a classic terrain trap, and if the snow is anything except stable you should not be here.

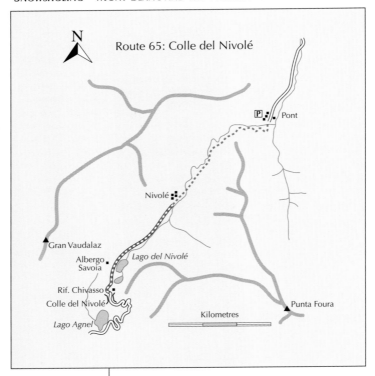

Head up to the Nivolé lakes, which will be snow-covered, next to the road opposite the Albergo Savoia, only open in summer. Perched up on a hill to the south is the Rifugio Chivasso, 2606m. Continue up past this to the Colle del Nivolé just beyond. Return by the same route.

66: Rifugio Benevolo, 2285m, and Punta Calabre, 3445m

Starting point	Thumel (or further down the road depending on the snow)
Starting altitude	1880m
Summit altitude	Rifugio Benevolo 2285m, Punta Calabre 3445m
Altitude gain	405m to Rifugio Benevolo, plus 1160m to summit
Time	2h30 to the hut (more if you can't drive to Thumel), 6h round trip to the summit from the hut, plus 1h30 to descend to Thumel
Grade	to hut 2, to summit G4
Aspect	W, N
Map	1:25,000 IGC 102 Valsavarenche, Val di Rhêmes, Valgrisenche; 1:50,000 Kompass Carta Turistica 86 Gran Paradiso
Accommodation	Rifugio Benevolo Tel: 016643375/ 0165 936143. Open mid-March to mid-May
Public transport	Bus Aosta–Rhêmes Notre Dame

Access: From Aosta drive to Villeneuve then up the Val di Rhêmes. Be sure to look over the bridge in Introd and also to admire the fabulous old houses of this village. Go past Rhêmes Notre Dame to park at the end of the road – depending on the snow this will be either at Bruil, Pelaud or Thumel.

The Rifugio Benevolo enjoys a privileged position among a cirque of beautiful glaciated peaks, none of them too steep or high, several of which can be envisaged on snowshoes after a night at the hut. Most of them form the frontier with France and views from the summits are spectacular. The Punta Calabre is probably the most amenable and offers a walk in splendid surroundings without any undue difficulty. However, this is glaciated terrain, and the usual precautions must be taken for glacier travel.

This is a popular venue for ski tourers and the hut is likely to be busy. Being Italian, the food is usually

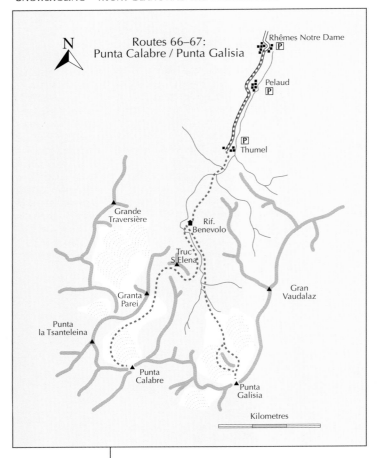

Routes 66–67:
Punta Calabre / Punta Galisia

N

Rhêmes Notre Dame
P

Pelaud
P

P
Thumel

Grande
Traversière

Rif.
Benevolo

Truc
S.Elena

Granta
Parei

Gran
Vaudalaz

Punta
la Tsanteleina

Punta
Calabre

Punta
Galisia

Kilometres

excellent and the ambience lively. Once out on the hill you will soon find the quiet and tranquility of the mountains.

From the summit you will be looking down into the Vanoise National Park, which adjoins the Gran Paradiso Park. To the west is the fine summit of La Grande

Sassière, whilst to the north are distant views of the Mont Blanc massif. In front of you the awe-inspiring cliffs of the Granta Parei complete this splendid panorama.

It should be noted that the Punta Calabre is also known as the Punta de Bazel, and on the French map of the area has only this name. In fact, the Roc du Fond, to the east of the Punta Calabre, is called the Punta Calabre on the French map, so be sure you know which summit you are aiming for.

Route

From Thumel follow the valley, taking the true left side of the river. Flat at first, the route steepens as you approach Alp Lavassey. Cross to the other side of the river wherever you can. Above, the Rifugio Benevolo is visible, and steepish slopes take you there in a short time.

The next day head directly south along the broad valley and up relatively gentle terrain, flanked on the right by the impressive cliffs of the Granta Parei. Your route takes you under the south slopes of Truc S. Elena and onto the long Ghiacciaio di Tsanteleynaz. Going south-east head up, skirting west around the rocks at pt 3293 then up south-west to the summit of the Punta Calabre.

Descend by the same route more or less, although you could vary the way down from the summit, taking the best snow.

Small snow-slides are often indicators of changes in temperature

67: Punta Galisia, 3346m

Access: From Aosta
drive to Villeneuve
then up the Val di
Rhêmes; past
Rhêmes Notre Dame
to park at the end of
the road, near
Thumel.

Starting point	Rifugio Benevolo
Starting altitude	2285m
Summit altitude	3346m
Altitude gain	1061m
Time	6h round trip
Grade	G4
Aspect	N
Map	1:25,000 IGC 102 Valsavarenche, Val di Rhêmes, Valgrisenche; 1:50,000 Kompass Carta Turistica 86 Gran Paradiso
Accommodation	Rifugio Benevolo Tel: 016643375/ 0165 936143. Open mid-March to mid-May
Public transport	Bus Aosta–Rhêmes Notre Dame

Punta Galisia is another option from the Benevolo hut. It gives great views of the Vanoise region to the south, dominated by the Grande Aiguille Rousse, whilst eastwards is the Gran Paradiso range.

Again this peak is glaciated, and the glacier can be quite crevassed, so care is needed. Ask at the hut for advice on conditions, and if the glacier is very open do not choose this objective.

Route
From the Benevolo hut (see Route 66) go south-east then south following either side of the valley gorge, whichever is easiest. At the end of the gorge follow undulating terrain and eventually set foot on the Lavassey Glacier and climb this towards the rognon (rock) at 2955m. Pass this on the right or the left depending on snow cover – the majority of ski tracks are likely to indicate the best way. Beware of crevasses in this area.

The Punta Galisia summit is soon attained above on the Franco-Italian border. Return by the same route.

68: Punta della Croce, 2478m

Starting point	Car park just before the col, opposite Les Genzianas bar
Starting altitude	1941m
Summit altitude	2478m
Altitude gain	537m
Time	4h30–5h round trip
Grade	2
Aspect	N, E
Map	1:25,000 IGC 107 Monte Bianco; 1:50,000 IGC 3 Gran Paradiso (only partly)

Access: From Aosta take the road towards Courmayeur as far as Morgex. Turn off left to go over the river and up to the Colle San Carlo.

The Colle San Carlo is a good place to go when the snow level is high and you want a walk that is not too long but at reasonable altitude. The col is at 1951m and is kept open throughout the winter. Of course this does not mean that there won't be snow on the road but,

Approaching the subsidiary summit pt 2348 near Punta della Croce

267

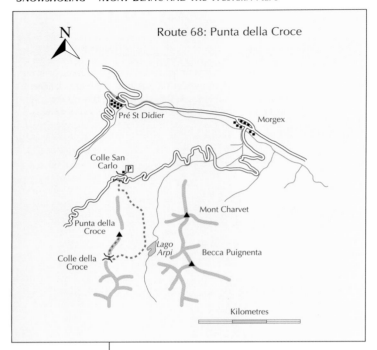

Route 68: Punta della Croce

N

Pré St Didier

Morgex

Colle San Carlo

P

Mont Charvet

Punta della Croce

Lago Arpi

Becca Puignenta

Colle della Croce

Kilometres

Further Options

If you take the trail signed to the Colle della Croce you can follow the summer path which traverses around the summit of pt 2348. When you arrive on the east slopes, however, this traverse will become impracticable or at least unpleasant, and you ▶

equipped with chains or snow-tyres, you can get there whatever.

From the col there are various options, of which the Punta della Croce is the best, but a visit here will certainly not disappoint, regardless of where you end up. The area is situated directly south-east of the Monte Bianco massif and consequently the Punta della Croce is an exceptional viewpoint. Even if you do not go to the summit, you'll be treated to fine views of the massif from the valley trail.

The Arpi Lake is popular and there is likely to be a good track leading there. Onwards to the Colle della Croce is bit steeper, and this slope leads you to the rounded summit ridge with an ancient fort near the top.

Route

Take the trail which goes south into the forest. After about 0.5km of flat track there is a junction. To the left is signed the Lago Arpi, and to the right the Colle della Croce. Despite the fact that the col is your objective take the left-hand trail. This leads round under the summit into a cwm formed by various summits. At the lake you need to head up to the west to the col. Although these slopes are quite steep, it is possible to find a gentle way through, depending on the snow depth. Once at the col turn right (north) and go up the crest to the Punta della Croce summit. Return by the same route.

can then make your way west up the rounded, sparsely forested shoulder to the lowest point on the summit ridge. This gives equally good views as the Punta Croce. However, this way should be avoided in anything except very stable snow conditions, as it crosses several slopes which regularly avalanche.

69: Monte della Saxe, 2524m

Starting point	Villair Superiore
Starting altitude	1327m
Summit altitude	2348m
Altitude gain	1021m
Time	7h round trip
Grade	2/3
Aspect	S
Map	1:25,000 IGC 107 Monte Bianco Courmayeur; 1:50,000 IGC 4 Monte Bianco
Public transport	Bus Aosta–Courmayeur

A gem! Whilst it is quite an arduous hike up from Courmayeur to the Monte della Saxe, this whale-back ridge is such a superb place that the pain is soon forgotten. The forest track may or may not be visible in the snow, and you will just have to find the best route. Above the forest the traverse across to the Rifugio Bertone, which is closed in winter, can be a little delicate, and if the snowpack is not stable this walk should be saved for another day. However, once the hut is reached just a short climb remains before you suffer the visual

Access: From Aosta drive to Courmayeur and park as near to Villair Superiore as possible.

onslaught of the Mont Blanc massif seen in all its splendour from this grand belvedere. From Mont Blanc itself, with the Peutrey arête in profile, to the Grandes Jorasses right in front of you, to Mont Dolent guarding the head of the Val Ferret, to the steep slopes of Mont Chétif above Courmayeur, this view can't be bettered. Stroll along to the rounded highpoint and enjoy.

Route
From Villair Superiore the forest track leading north-east is gentle at first until, after about 20 minutes, you see the signpost directing you left to the Rifugio Bertone. Try to stick to the summer path if possible, although deep snow-cover may make this difficult. At around 1800m you must traverse left (west) to then ascend to the hut above at 2000m. This traverse is short but requires care, and can only be envisaged in stable snow conditions as this is a steep and long slope. Sometimes it is best to go high, up to a cliff, before traversing.

Nearing the tree-line

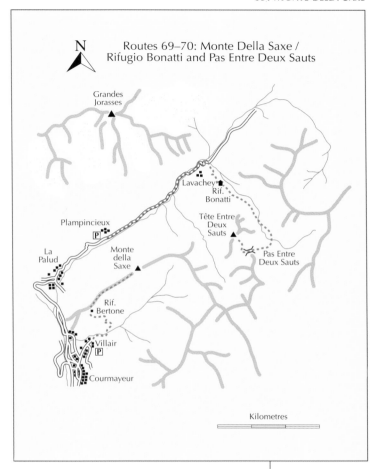

Routes 69–70: Monte Della Saxe / Rifugio Bonatti and Pas Entre Deux Sauts

From the hut take the obvious steep south-facing slope above (again, be careful, as this slope too can be avalanche prone) to reach the rounded shoulder stretching on delightfully to the summit of Monte della Saxe. Descend by the same route.

70: Rifugio Walter Bonatti, 2025m, and Tête Entre Deux Sauts, 2729m

Note: on the new Swiss 1:25,000 map of this area the 'Sauts' is marked 'Sex'.

Access: From Aosta drive to Courmayeur. From here you can drive up the Val Ferret as far as Plampincieux (or later in the season to Lavachey).

Starting point	Plampincieux or Lavachey, if the road is open
Starting altitude	1550m
Summit altitude	Rifugio Walter Bonatti 2025m, Tête Entre Deux Sauts 2729m
Altitude gain	475m to hut, 704m to Tête Entre Deux Sauts
Time	2h30 to hut, 4h round trip hut to summit
Grade	to hut 1, to summit 2/3
Aspect	N, S, E, W
Map	1:25,000 IGC 107 Monte Bianco Courmayeur; 1:50,000 IGC 4 Monte Bianco
Accommodation	Rifugio Walter Bonatti Tel: 0165 869055
Public transport	Bus Aosta–Courmayeur–Plampincieux

There are lots of reasons for doing the Tête Entre Deux Sauts, but the most compelling has got to be the Rifugio Walter Bonatti. Who could resist a beautiful new 'hut' (I use the term loosely, as this hut beats many hotels) built in traditional Valdotain (Aosta) style, lavishly decorated with photos taken by Bonatti himself during his incredible career as an alpinist and photographer, with duvets on the beds, serving a fabulous five-course Italian dinner every night and offering a 'copious' breakfast? You could put it at the top of the worst scree slope and it would still be worth going! In this case it is situated just a gentle walk up the valley right opposite the Grandes Jorasses and gives access to several fine walks.

The Italian Val Ferret alone provides a pleasant *sor-*

tie in the winter, formed as it is on its north side by the huge summits of the Grandes Jorasses, Aiguille de Léschaux and Aiguille de Triolet, and, at its head, the splendid Mont Dolent, the boundary of France, Switzerland and Italy.

You could make this a real gastronomic extravaganza by spending a lazy day approaching the hut via the Val Ferret, with a long lunch at Lavachey, renowned for its polenta which, when cooked by Italians is actually very good, then finally wobbling up to the hut.

From the hut views are magnificent – the Mont Blanc massif in all its glory, with the Jorasses taking pride of place. The Tête Entre Deux Sauts could feasibly be done in a long day from the valley, but only a masochist would pass by the refuge and not be tempted to stay.

The Tête Entre Deux Sauts is a viable proposition only when the snow is reasonably stable and not too icy, and the avalanche risk is not high. The hut wardens will advise on this. The climb to the summit is interesting and varied, and the summit vista is outstanding – from the steep Brenva face of Mont Blanc and the spectacular Peutrey Arête, with the dark spire of the Aiguille Noire de Peutrey, all the way along the frontier ridge featuring, amongst other peaks, the characteristic tooth of the Dent du Géant. Stretching away to the south-west is the Val Veny snaking down from the Col de la Seigne, bordering with France.

If the Tête itself is too icy it may well be possible to do the small subsidiary summit of pt 2612 just above the Pas Entre Deux Sauts, which is itself a good objective. It is possible to do the Tour of the Tête Entre Deux Sauts by descending from the col into the Armina valley and then traversing around and back to the hut path, but this is only feasible in very stable conditions and is long and hazardous.

Route
Wander up the valley to Lavachey, taking care to avoid the cross-country ski pistes. There are special pedestrian paths, but it is far more interesting to make your way

Arriving at the Rifugio Bonatti

along one side or the other, well away from the groomed trails. The best way is probably to walk a little way next to the pistes then cross the river by the bridge at Meyenzet, which leads to a lovely flat walk along the golf course as far as Lavachey, with its popular café and sunloungers for those who'd like to do some bronzing.

Follow the main track beyond Lavachey up two hairpins then take the signed path into the forest. After half an hour there is a junction, signed right to the Armina valley and left to the refuge. Take the left-hand path, which continues more steeply until it reaches the treeline. Not far above is the hut.

The Pas Entre Deux Sauts is reached by following the Malatra valley up to the steeper slopes at the head of the cwm. Here head west and up to the col. Above are the east slopes of the Tête Entre Deux Sauts. Although in some conditions the east face may be feasible on snowshoes, the most likely route is via the south-east ridge. This is accessed by going up or around pt 2612. If you can get to the ridge then it is a gentle climb up to the summit. In icy conditions crampons may be necessary – but remember that you have to be able to get down safely. Pt 2612 itself can be ascended either directly from the col or by descending a little then taking the southwest shoulder to the top.

Descend by the same route, obviously calling into the hut for a cappuccino or celebratory genepy before continuing the descent to Lavachey. When you reach the valley, for variety you could return on the other side of the Val Ferret by crossing the bridge and returning via Pra Sec and Tronchey, but do be careful to keep off the groomed cross-country ski pistes.

Further Options

To do the Tour of the Tête Entre Deux Sauts you must find a slope from the Pas Entre Deux Sauts that you're happy to descend into the neighbouring Armina valley. The summer path is not much help here, as it takes a long traverse that is rarely practicable on snowshoes. The gully leading directly south-west from the col may be feasible. However, the slope

The Pas and Tête Entre Deux Sauts

is slightly convex, so it is difficult to see from above. If you go down here you must be careful and be prepared to come back up if it gets too steep. Clearly in anything but very stable snow conditions you should not go this way.

Once in the valley flat ground leads to a deep valley, and you must take a traverse above this. It may be necessary to remove snowshoes here. Remember that if these slopes are hot, which they are likely to be by the time you get there, they can be very risky for wet avalanches and full-depth slides.

Above the alpage of Armina take the easiest line in a descending traverse to Secheron, from where the path is more obvious, around to rejoin the hut path.

The Col de Malatra is another destination on snowshoes, situated at the northern extremity of the cwm. Note that this is off the 1:25,000 map, but is on the Swiss map Carte Nationale de la Suisse 1365 Grand St Bernard.

APPENDIX 1:
Useful Terms and Glossary

VOCABULARY – WEATHER

English	French	Italian	German
weather	temps	tempo	wetter
forecast	prévision	bolletino	vohersage
hot	chaud	caldo	heiss
cold	froid	freddo	kalt
sunny	ensoleillé	soleggiato	sonnig
rainy	pluvieux	piovos	regnerisch
windy	venté	ventoso	windig
cloudy	nuageux	nuvoloso	bewölkt
foggy	brouillard	nebbioso	neblig
stormy	orageux	temporalesco	stürmisch
snowy	enneigé	nevoso	schneereich,
temperature	température	temperatura	temperatur
changeable	variable	variabile	veränderlich verschneit
thunder	tonnère	tuono	donner
lightening	éclair	fulmine	blitz
gusts/gales	rafales	raffiche di vento	bö, windstoss
white out	jour blanc	luce abbacinante	verlieren der sicht
ice	glace	ghiaccio	eis
verglace	verglas	ghiaccio vivo, verglace	glatteis
hail	grêle	grandine	hagel
avalanche	avalanche	valanga	lawine
freezing	glacial	congelamento	eisig, eiskalt
starry	étoillé	stellato	sternklar

VOCABULARY – EMERGENCY

Help!	au secours!	aiuto!	hilfe!
Accident	accident	incidente	unfall

English	French	Italian	German
Emergency	urgence	emergenza	notfall
Stop!	halte	stop (alt)	stop
Quick	vite	presto	schnell
Be careful!	faites attention	attenzione	achtung
Rescue	secours	soccorso	retten,rettung
Helicopter	hélicoptère	elicottero	hubschrauber
Ambulance	ambulance	ambulanza	ambulanz
Hospital	hôpital	ospedale	spital
Doctor	medecin/docteur	dottore, medico	doktor, arzt
SOS phone	téléphone d'urgence	telefono di soccorso	nottelefon
Heart attack	crise cardiaque	attacco di cuore, infarto	herzanfall, herzinfarkt
Stroke	hémiplégie	attacco	schlaganfall
Broken arm	bras cassé	braccio rotto	armbruch,
Broken leg	jambe cassée	gambe rotta	beinbruch
Asthma	crise d'asthma	attacco d'asma	asthmaanfall

GLOSSARY

The following terms may need some explanation. They are used throughout the book.

Col: a pass or a saddle. In German it is usually 'joch' and in Italian 'colle' or 'bocca'.

Alpage: a summer farm usually above the tree-line. Cattle are brought up here for the months of July and August to graze.

Cwm/corrie/combe: this is a basin surrounded on three sides by hills or mountains. It can be steep-sided or more gently rounded. Often there is a lake in the basin and a stream flows out of the unenclosed side, down into the valley.

Rognon: a rock island or buttress, standing alone in a glacier. These are often landmarks for glacier travel, and can be crucial in the fog.

APPENDIX 2:
Bibliography

Avalanche Safety for Skiers and Climbers, Tony Daffern, published by The Mountaineers, 1999

The Essential Snowshoer, Marianne Zwosta, published by Ragged Mountain Press, 1998

Guide des Traces d'Animaux, P Bang and P Dahlström, published by Delachaux et Niestlé, 1996

La Raquete à Neige, Jean-Marc Lamory, published by Didier Richard, 1995

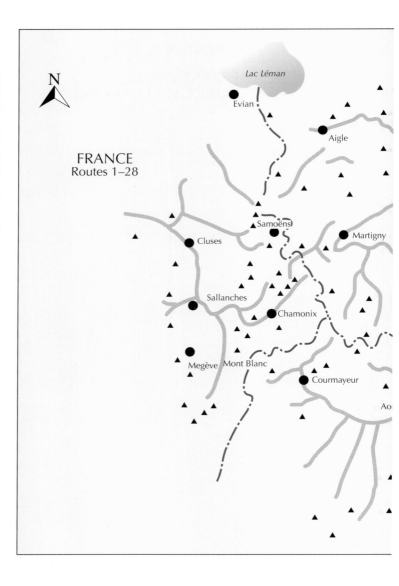

CHAMONIX AND THE
SURROUNDING AREA

Sierre

Sion

Zinal

SWITZERLAND
Routes 29–57

Arolla

Zermatt

Grand Combin   Matterhorn   Monte
Rosa

Aosta

ITALY
Routes 58–70

NOTES

NOTES

LISTING OF CICERONE GUIDES

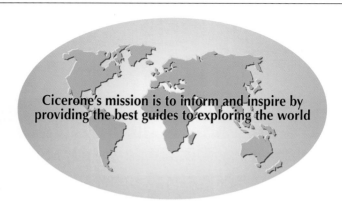

Cicerone's mission is to inform and inspire by providing the best guides to exploring the world

Since its foundation over 30 years ago, Cicerone has specialised in publishing guidebooks and has built a reputation for quality and reliability. It now publishes nearly 300 guides to the major destinations for outdoor enthusiasts, including Europe, UK and the rest of the world.

Written by leading and committed specialists, Cicerone guides are recognised as the most authoritative. They are full of information, maps and illustrations so that the user can plan and complete a successful and safe trip or expedition – be it a long face climb, a walk over Lakeland fells, an alpine traverse, a Himalayan trek or a ramble in the countryside.

With a thorough introduction to assist planning, clear diagrams, maps and colour photographs to illustrate the terrain and route, and accurate and detailed text, Cicerone guides are designed for ease of use and access to the information.

If the facts on the ground change, or there is any aspect of a guide that you think we can improve, we are always delighted to hear from you.

Cicerone Press
2 Police Square Milnthorpe Cumbria LA7 7PY
Tel:01539 562 069 Fax:01539 563 417
e-mail:info@cicerone.co.uk web:www.cicerone.co.uk